To John Carver Harris,
who insisted this book be written;
and to Avilés and St. Augustine,
sister cities which Menéndez loved.

FOREWORD

AT LONG LAST, Pedro Menéndez de Avilés, settler of Florida and first founding father of our nation, has been made the subject of a modern biography in the English language. Not since 1905 and the publication of the second volume of Woodbury Lowery's *The Spanish Settlements in the United States,* has the Adelantado's extraordinary career been recounted in book form in this country. For over half a century, the Lowery work has been the standard source to which we have turned for enlightenment about the man who conquered Florida, built our nation's first permanent settlement and missions, and ruled for nearly a decade over most of what is now the United States.

How did it happen that such a man, such a giant in the American epic, has otherwise fallen into academic as well as popular oblivion? There are at least two reasons. For one thing, it is a truism that the victors write the histories, and in Menéndez' case, the Spanish Crown that he represented lost out eventually in its contest with England for suzerainty over the North American continent. Since the time of Parson Weems, and certainly that of George Bancroft, American historians have been English-oriented in their approach to the nation's beginnings, and as a consequence, the contributions of Spain to those beginnings have been obscured under the supervening grandeur of Pilgrims, Virginians, and Carolinians. It is no accident that most Americans seem to have learned in school that our permanent history began at Plymouth Rock, which, inconveniently for the victors' point of view, came into being fifty-five years after Menéndez' settlement at Saint Augustine.

A second reason for the neglect shown to Pedro Menéndez can be found in the *leyenda negra,* the Black Legend, which came to surround his name in France and England, and later in this country, as a result of the Adelantado's destruction of the French force at Fort Caroline (at the mouth of the St. John's), and his slaughter soon after of Jean Ribault and his compatriots at Matanzas Inlet. Both events occurred in the fall of 1565, and were occasioned by orders Menéndez carried from King Philip II of Spain. Discharge of his mandate, military necessity, inability

FLORIDA'S

MENÉNDEZ

CAPTAIN GENERAL OF THE OCEAN SEA

by

Albert Manucy

The St. Augustine Historical Society
St. Augustine, Florida

Printed by
The E. O. Painter Printing Co., DeLeon Springs, Florida

to feed the French captives from his meagre stores — over a hundred Spaniards would die from starvation during the first winter — these appear to have been the reasons which led Menéndez to carry out his instructions so completely. If religion was one of the reasons deployed by Menéndez for ridding Florida of the French, then so much the worse for his use of religion, but the battle itself, as Albert Manucy agrees in this fine narrative, was not essentially a religious battle.

The contest to gain a foothold in Florida is not the story of the foothold itself, nor is it by any means the story of Pedro Menéndez. In these pages, the reader will learn that the Adelantado was more than a great seaman and military tactician. He was a builder and a missionary. He succeeded where six earlier Spanish expeditions had failed. He made a city and he planted the Cross. Those are his supreme, his unforgettable accomplishments. The day he strode ashore at the site called Nombre de Dios (Name of God), and named his settlement Saint Augustine, he inaugurated a new epic in the history of western man. And the fruits of that epic could be seen only ninety years later, at Nombre de Dios, and at thirty other missions on the coast and in the interior, where 26,000 North American Indians had learned Christianity and the rudiments of European arts and crafts.

This is the man about whom Mr. Manucy has written so capably. I can think of no other historian more qualified to tell the tale. Since 1938, as an historian for the National Park Service at the Castillo de San Marcos and elsewhere, the author has been engaged in the work of collecting, calendaring, comparing, and critically reviewing all of the known documentary material relating to Menéndez' life and career. No one knows those materials better than he; no one is more intimately acquainted with the man whose story they tell.

The present book is a narrative summary of the author's findings, and a portent, we may well hope, of the full length, definitive study that he plans to give us later.

University of Florida   Michael V. Gannon

CONTENTS

PEDRO MENÉNDEZ DE AVILÉS

This 18th century engraving is from the Titian portrait of Don Pedro.
(From *Retratos de los Españoles Ilustres*, Madrid, 1791.)

In the King's Service

THE SEA was quiet. A calm, cool morning it was, the mists not yet fled from the sun. In the light air, the coast guard vessels drifted, sails furled and sweeps at rest. Behind them, the harbor was a cleft in green hills that swept upward from the rocky coast. This was Galicia.

The three boats were *pataches*, small but fast row-sailers, fine for the coast patrol. Their mission was against corsairs, of course, for in the 1540's the Spanish coasts were never free of these sea robbers; and fighting them was a fair way to make a living in the King's Service.

Or so it seemed to the youth. His name was Pedro Menéndez, and he captained one of the little ships. He watched a trio of freighters making slow passage to the next port. Obviously there would be a wedding soon. On the hindmost ship was a bridal party, happily escorting a young woman to her betrothed. Ribald jests were bandied about as this craft, her rails heavy with people, nosed past the patrol.

Then out of nowhere loomed the corsairs, sails spread and oars flashing as they came on after the freighters. There were four attackers — a ship and three swift *zabras*, the Biscayan frigates of that day. The powerful *zabras* soon overtook the bride's crowded transport.

With mounting concern, Pedro saw it all. These were French enemies. He knew what would happen to the bride and the other women.

"Come!" he shouted to the men in the *pataches*. "We go to save the maiden and her women. Or we die!"

Don't be a fool, their faces told him. "We are badly out-numbered," they muttered.

So only his craft pursued the pirates, he alone with his fifty men, relying on them and his own clever strength, and on the nimbleness of his vessel. It was a daring thing, and done with a flourish: with the shrill of the fife and the beat of the drum, and the pennants hoisted aloft. The oarsmen plied the blades with a will that fluttered the pennants astern. Then the sails were loosed in the promise of a livening breeze.

9

Seeing a lone *patache* approach, the Frenchmen waited, sniffing another easy victory. The three *zabras* clustered around their prize. Their ship was now a league away, outdistanced during the chase.

The incongruous sight and sound as the *patache* came on — fife whistling, drum thundering, flags flying, and a little company of armed men on her deck — entertained the corsairs. Out of curiosity they fell quiet as she neared, and her young captain picked up the trumpet.

"Yield this prize," Pedro shouted, "else I will hang you all!"

Of course they laughed at him, this cocky figure whose beard could not hide his youth. When the roar subsided, one of them mocked him.

"Why sure, Captain, sir. Just you come aboard and take it. We'll give it to *you*, all right!"

Two *zabras* moved to grapple the *patache*.

There was nothing to do but run, so run he did. And, as the old account says, the first *zabra* was faster than the second, and the *patache* faster than either. Pedro ran until he had well separated the two pursuers. Then he turned fiercely upon the foremost and took her. Next he put half his fighting men aboard this captive and used both her and his own vessel to capture the second *zabra*.

The crew of the third, still guarding the bride, saw him coming back. Suddenly they realized he intended to carry out his promise of the hangman. In quick council they reached a logical decision: the prize should be yielded; and without risking another encounter with this madman, they should depart. And they did.

Pedro Menéndez was born to adventure. He came into the world at the time when Spain was on the threshold of great conquests beyond the Atlantic. His was one of the ancient families in the old kingdom of Asturias, and a bravely prolific one. Juan Alfonso Sánchez de Avilés, his father, had served the Catholic Kings gallantly in the war of Granada; and upon marriage to María Alonso de Arango, he begot twenty children.

Pedro was among the younger sons. Doña María brought him into this life at the little town of Avilés, which is on a pleasant estuary of the north coast. Avilés was thus doubly his name, as it had been for his forefathers. It was a good name, and it sets him apart from others called Pedro Menéndez, a fine-sounding cognomen very popular amongst the Spanish.

Pedro Menéndez de Avilés! His first years were spent in the green highlands of Asturias, within sight of the sea; which, like a lover, forever beckons with unspeakable promises. Nor did the boy long resist the call.

He was still a child when his father died. The family was not wealthy, and when Doña María married again, Pedro was sent to live with a relative who promised to see to his education. He and his benefactor did not see eye to eye, and he ran away from home. Understandably the family was alarmed; but six months went by before he was discovered — or let himself be found — in Valladolid and taken back, more or less willingly, to his foster home.

It was not at all certain he would stay. For he was a restless, intelligent lad, mature beyond his years. Perhaps it was this maturity which inspired his guardian (or more likely the lady of the household) to betroth Pedro to a distant cousin, a ten-year-old charmer named Ana María. She was the girl he would marry, when they were both grown; and she was the one to whom he would be a true husband — as true, that is, as one can be whose mistress is the sea. No maidenly wiles could long divert a lad who longed for the salt wind of the Atlantic.

So he went off again, now to fight in one of the incessant wars with France. For two years he served in a small armada against the French corsairs who harried the coasts and the shipping of his country. The two years grew him into a man, with a man's ambition to command his own vessel; and when the time was out, he made his way home with plans to sell a bit of his inheritance and build a vessel of his own. His people begged him to stay, to leave the sea; and doubtless Ana María added her voice; but his dream was brighter than theirs, and so effectively did he tell of it that many kinsfolk sailed with him when the boat was ready.

The swift *patache* was superlative for a confident young man in search of adventure. And she was the craft that carried him to victory that pleasant morning off Galicia.

The deeds of Pedro Menéndez soon became matter for conversation in the waterfront wine shops of France and Spain, as well as in royal palaces. Depending upon one's viewpoint, Menéndez was a brash and ruthless foe who was destroying

PHILIP II, KING OF SPAIN 1556-1598
(From a portrait by Titian)

"freedom of the seas"; or he was a brave and talented leader who was freeing Spanish waters from piracy. Since he threatened the livelihood of so many sea ruffians, they continuously sought a way to kill him. Whether in war or peace, he was in danger. This the Spanish rulers knew, and agreed it was only fair that he be free to fight back at his enemies. Besides, as he seemed to win all his battles, it was in the national interest to keep him employed.

It was also good business. The Crown authorized him to hunt corsairs twelve months a year, if he wanted to, and in peacetime or in war. Legitimate prizes that he took on the high seas would be his; and if he seized contraband or smugglers' goods, he would collect a legal share.

As expected, Pedro not only survived, but thrived on the murderous attempts of his enemies. And the fame he won led to great honors.

In those days, Philip II was a young prince making ready to marry the Queen of England. Philip's father, the Emperor Charles V, who had once thought to marry her himself, made the arrangements, seeing this as a good way to get England on his side in the current trouble with France.

The Queen was Mary I, thirty-eight-year-old daughter of Henry VIII and Catherine of Aragón. The betrothal was the most recent of Mary's rather long string of affiancements in the name of diplomacy (starting with her engagement to the Emperor himself when she was only six). All, for this reason or that, had failed to end in matrimony. Though Charles had found it best to wed himself to another, he liked this woman. He had been a real help to her during Henry's shocking divorce of her mother, and in the difficult aftermath when Mary's own life was in danger. Half-Spanish herself, wanting to please the Emperor Charles and perhaps have his help in the restoration of Catholicism to England, she overruled the strident objections voiced by many of her subjects and firmly announced her intention to marry the Spanish Prince Philip. Besides, for one her age, if ever she was to enjoy the benefactions of the married state, there was no time to lose.

Philip, a dutiful son, raised no notable objection to marrying a woman eleven years older than he. With characteristic attention to detail he planned the journey to London, considered the multifarious aspects of the alliance with Mary, and made a list of the people who could best serve him on this occasion.

One of them was Don Pedro Menéndez de Avilés.

By 1554, the year of Philip's wedding, Menéndez was thirty-five years old. He had had some twenty years of experience on the sea as a leader of men in a highly dangerous profession — warfare against crafty, ruthless mariners who lived by the law of force and whose guns and seamanship were often as good as his own.

He was not handsome. But his compact, muscular build showed him to be a man of action, and the sun-on-water lines around his eyes and his manner of walk marked him as a sailor. He had a small head, held quite erect; his hair, half curly despite a short cut, framed a high, round forehead. The beard was also trimmed rather short. Between widespread dark eyes there were habitual creases; his nose was overlong and his mouth too small; but the eyes under the straight brows reflected the man's intelligence. He smiled easily and could, on occasion, laugh at himself as well as others (which is a rare talent). In short, he was good to be with, for though he had a ready tongue, he was also able to listen. However, as one close to him said, he was a great friend of his own opinion.

Philip had named Menéndez to serve in the retinue as counselor, and thus he did serve very well, for he got on with the English and quickly became a favorite of Queen Mary. One suspects, nevertheless, that the sailor was not sorry to have his prince properly wedded and himself free once again to depart the formality of the royal circle.

On the day after the marriage, he set out to take the official news of the affair back to the Spanish court. Though the trip began casually enough, it turned out to be an exciting one. On a freight *zabra* enroute to northern Spain he found passage for himself and the six crack arquebusiers of his guard. There was a prosperous wind.

But one afternoon only four leagues from Laredo on the Asturian coast, they were spotted by a pair of corsair vessels. Expecting the usual easy conquest of a merchantman, the pirates came alongside to board. The terrified crew wanted to surrender rather than risk being cut to pieces in a fight, but Menéndez would have none of this.

The helmsman craftily thought to settle the matter by slipping away from the helm. The vessel began to fall off the wind; in a moment she would be completely vulnerable. Menéndez himself sprang to the tiller, and there he stayed. For

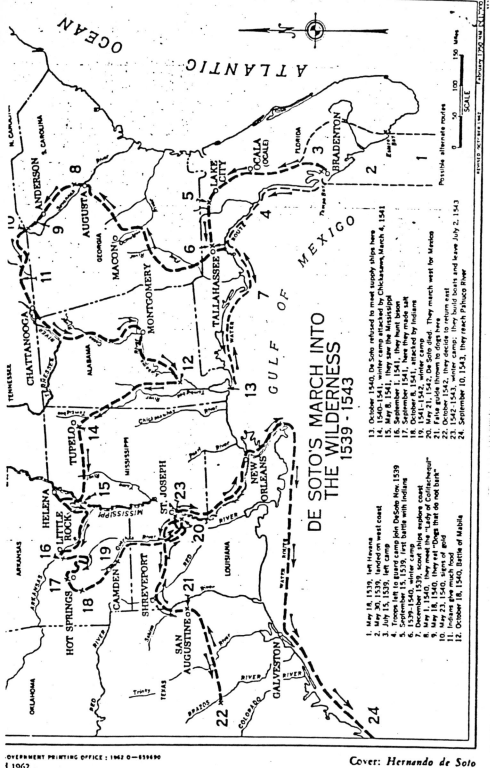

DE SOTO'S MARCH INTO THE WILDERNESS
1539 - 1543

1. May 18, 1539, left Havana
2. May 30, 1539, landed on west coast
3. July 15, 1539, left camp
4. September 15, 1539, first battle with Indians
5. Troops left to guard camp join DeSoto Nov. 1539
6. 1539-1540, winter camp
7. December 1539, scout ships explore coast
8. May 1, 1540, they meet the "Lady of Cofitachequi"
9. May 21, 1540, they eat "Dogs that do not bark"
10. May 23, 1540, signs of gold
11. Indians give much food
12. October 18, 1540, Battle of Mabila

13. October 1540, De Soto refused to meet supply ships here
14. 1540-1541, winter camp attacked by Chickasaws, March 4, 1541
15. May 8, 1541, they saw the Mississippi
16. September 1, 1541, they hunt bison
17. September 1541, here they made salt
18. October 8, 1541, attacked by Indians
19. 1541-1542, winter camp
20. May 21, 1542, De Soto died. They march west for Mexico
21. False guide thrown to dogs here
22. October 1542, they decide to return east
23. 1542-1543, winter camp; they build boats and leave July 2, 1543
24. September 10, 1543, they reach Pahuco River

Possible alternate routes

SCALE
0   50   100   150   Miles

REVISED OCTOBER 1942
February 1762 NPS INTERIOR

Cover: *Hernando de Soto*

GOVERNMENT PRINTING OFFICE : 1962 O—639690
1962

protection from the bolts and bullets of the enemy, he had the men pile mattresses into a barricade. His arquebusiers stayed near.

The corsairs held a low opinion of army arquebusiers, and so made fine targets of themselves for these marksmen who, as often as not, hit where they aimed. Surprised, the corsairs backed off. Oncoming darkness and fear of the doughty marksmen decided them against another try.

So Menéndez soon stepped ashore at Laredo. From there he made his way to Valladolid and handed over the royal dispatches.

About a year after Philip's marriage, Charles V abdicated the throne of empire. Philip became King of Spain and of the possessions in America, Italy, and the Netherlands. He also inherited the hostilities with France, a matter which was to occupy his mind for many a month. Menéndez likewise became involved, for in 1557 the new King put him in charge of a convoy taking supplies and reinforcements to the battlefront. Despite an encounter with a large French fleet headed by the notorious Jacques le Clerc, *alias* "Peg Leg," Menéndez landed money and men safely at Calais in record time.

This ability to move rapidly and decisively was typical of Pedro Menéndez. So was his tendency to interpret orders loosely at times. If he thought it best to disregard instructions, he did so without qualms, utterly sure of his own good judgment and the favor of Providence. It seems never to have occurred to him that if either failed, his head would be the forfeit.

An instance in point was the convoy from Laredo to Antwerp in 1558. He was to take four warships and escort six freight *zabras* to King Philip, who was again calling for supplies in Flanders. It was a long trip past the hostile French shoreline, and every port sheltered corsairs who knew he was coming.

When Menéndez got to Laredo, nothing was ready except four of the *zabras*. But the wind was right for him and wrong for the corsairs, so away he went with the quartet of freighters, not bothering to wait for the warships. By the time the corsairs could get out of their havens and look for him, he was already unloading in Antwerp.

He showed similar independence on a return convoy. Orders told him to take six vessels to Spain. The news that a French armada was blocking the route had stacked twenty-seven merchantmen in port. Although he had authority for only six vessels, he added the entire twenty-seven to the convoy.

15

As expected, the French fleet — and it was a strong one of twelve big galleons commanded by the Admiral of Normandy — came to meet them. At the lower end of the English Channel between the islands of Scilly and Ushant, and with plenty of sea room, Menéndez shepherded his convoy together, attacked, withdrew, feinted and dodged, and so confused the Frenchman that the convoy entered Laredo, so the account assures us, "without the loss of so much as a pin."

When at last the English decided to help their Queen's husband against the French, the task of convoying the troops across the Channel fell to Menéndez. From Dover to Calais the transports took horses, soldiers, and experts in the touchy techniques of explosive mining, to help in the siege of Saint Quentin. In addition, a number of English gentlemen made the crossing either on business or for adventure. Menéndez worked in concert with an English fleet, and so well did they operate together that the enemy forces were harmlessly bottled up in port.

I have already said that Queen Mary liked Don Pedro; this time, too, she was much pleased with him. So were the English gentlemen. In fact, such was his goodwill that Pedro Menéndez became a favorite and entertaining host. Many marvelled at these things, for they believed it impossible for Spaniard and Englishman to hit it off, either in work or in play.

As Saint Quentin's siege moved toward the climax, a strong armada made ready to leave Spain with reinforcements under the Prince De Eboli. The safe arrival of this expedition was vital. But as always, the route was flanked by eight hundred long miles of French coastline. Spanish intelligence confirmed reports of strong naval forces ready to waylay the convoy.

To cut down the odds, Philip ordered three squadrons to wait for De Eboli's ships as they came into the English Channel, and sail with them through the narrows to the destination.

The squadrons took their positions, awaiting the rendezvous. But as the time approached, the weather worsened. A terrific storm was in the making.

One of the three was English. "Let's get into port," urged their officers. But Pedro Menéndez saw the wind was coming straight from Spain, and it would blow De Eboli here whether he wanted to come or not.

"We disobey the King's orders if we let the enemy hit that convoy," he said. "I'm not going in."

This storm will scatter us all anyway, they told him. And then, seeing that his mind was made up, they asked him to order one — just one — of his ships into port. Plaintively they pointed out that when the Queen saw one of Don Pedro's ships in the haven, she would know the storm was really a bad one, and not berate her own sailors for coming in.

Arguments were useless, and at last two squadrons raced the gale to the nearest shelter. The third one, the crews grumbling and cursing their luck as seamen do, yet secretly proud that their skipper was a real deepwater man, rode out the tempest, keeping their position between Ushant and Scilly. This was a fine little armada of eight craft: two choice galleons, solid and swift, and the rest smaller, but fast and well-armed.

The storm blew itself out. Some days later, Menéndez climbed to the topsails for a look at the horizon. As he gazed to the south, the distant haze yielded a line of vessels stretched in a great crescent from east to west. The lookouts finally counted over eighty ships. Could this be De Eboli? Impossible. There were far too many ships. Then who was it?

Somebody said this must be a French fleet inbound from Newfoundland. The word spread like wildfire. The French! There would be prizes for the taking!

Menéndez was as pleased as anyone. Within minutes he had sketched the battle plan and tactical orders were going out.

Swiftly the gap was closing. A little more time and identification would be certain. A *patache* nosed out of the big fleet and coursed directly for his galleon. The moment he saw her, Menéndez cancelled the attack order. He recognized this *patache*. She was from Laredo. Her captain would be Diego Flores de Valdés, an old friend.

"You've cost us a lot of prizes," Menéndez said with mock disappointment as Captain Flores came alongside. "We thought you were French."

The Captain laughed and assured him this was a Spanish armada. Prince De Eboli was aboard the flagship with Captain General Diego de Mendoza; and the Admiral of the armada was none other than Pedro's own brother, Alvaro Sánchez de Avilés.

By now the first of the convoy was upon and around them. The word went to the helmsman and the galleon slipped through the white-gleaming sail forest, which was pushing steadily northward under the pressure of a fair wind. From van to rear guard the eighty ships stretched for a league, and in the last position Menéndez found the admiral's galleon—the *almiranta*—where his brother would be.

17

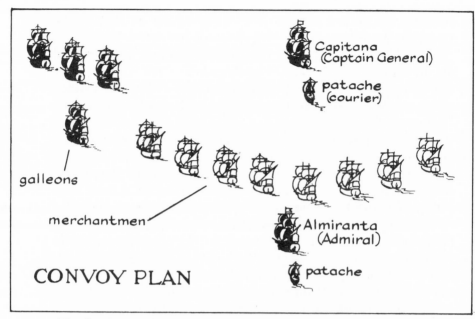

CONVOY PLAN

The flagship of the Captain General, commander of the convoy, led the van. The Admiral, second in command, sailed rearguard and shepherded the merchantmen. Off to the windward were other heavily armed galleons, ready to intercept the corsairs. Courier *pataches* stayed near the flagships. (After Guillén.)

The *almiranta* was a big vessel, her rails lined with curious soldiers. And there on the poop was Don Alvaro. Perhaps Menéndez remembered an earlier time when they had faced each other from tiny *pataches,* instead of the great ships they commanded this day.

His galleon took the new course neatly and was soon beside the *almiranta.* The two men exchanged salutes. Alvaro, speaking across the heaving water between them, greeted him like the affectionate older brother he was. His companions likewise shouted their greeting in a fine exchange of good spirits. Menéndez was a favorite and they were glad to see him, and seeing him meant that the cause of Spain was going well. Alvaro explained that the convoy carried six thousand troops, of whom four hundred were aboard the *almiranta.* The commanding colonel was among the gentlemen standing on the poop.

Menéndez soon said goodbye and gave orders to overtake the *capitana* or flagship far up in the van of this great fleet. Convoys are of course paced by the slowest craft, and any of the shepherding warships could literally sail rings around the plodding freighters. Nevertheless, one suspects that he had purposely

18

threaded his galleon through the entire convoy so that on his return to the vanguard he could show off her speed.

Rapidly she overhauled the banner-bedecked flagship, and did it with a nice display of seamanship. Once abreast, they dipped the flag and fired the guns, and Don Pedro and a dozen of his gentlemen dropped into a tender and crossed over to pay their respects to the Prince.

They met with a pleasant reception aboard the flagship, and the Prince talked over his plans for landing at Dartmouth, a few leagues east of Plymouth. Thence he would proceed to London to kiss Queen Mary's hand before going on to meet King Philip in Flanders. Some of the gentlemen would go along.

The disembarcation of the Prince and numerous nobles in his entourage took place as planned. A pair of *zabras* served to ferry the gentlemen from the fleet, which anchored well offshore. Menéndez personally assumed command of the one carrying the Prince, and thanks to a contrary wind and tide, had to spend the night in Dartmouth rather than return to the fleet.

The town was attractive. The houses were in tiers upon hillsides rising steeply from the water. The land-locked harbor, an estuary of the River Dart, was spacious. In the year 1485 the burgesses had received a royal grant to wall the town and install a chain across the harbor entrance. This defensive device was controlled by a capstan, housed in a strong tower on the shore. Normally the chain lay slack in the mud of the bottom; but in time of danger, men would turn the capstan, tautening the wrought-iron links and raising them into a barrier impassable for even the largest vessels.

The next morning, Menéndez lost no time in getting back to the fleet to talk with General Mendoza. The weather signs were bad. The armada must either find harbor or run well out to sea, because they were in for a dangerous side gale. They were situated in a great shoreline crescent called Lyme Bay. The coming weather would make it impossible to clear the long, dangerous hook of land at the far end of the crescent.

Unfortunately, it took a while to convince the pilots of the danger, and longer yet to get the big convoy under way. Rather than duck into port, the General decided to take the risk at sea. Philip needed this convoy delivered as soon as possible.

Meanwhile, Menéndez had moved his own squadron two leagues offshore, and was impatiently waiting for Mendoza to follow. But as the morning wore into afternoon and the wind increased and the sea roughened, the General's fleet was having a hard time of it.

It was four in the afternoon when Menéndez came to a decision. Leaving the safety of the open sea, he made for the laboring flagship, easing right up to her poop. Shouting over the gale, he told the General to put into the closest haven, which was Dartmouth.

By now Mendoza was fully aroused to the danger. Even a landsman could tell by the howl of the wind and the gathering gloom that trouble was coming. He accepted the instruction with alacrity and soon the fleet was converging on Dartmouth harbor.

Menéndez' swift vessels could already have reached it, but it seemed to him proper to act as rear guard and be sure that all the convoy was in first. It was an unlucky decision.

For as the flagship reached the narrow port entrance, the lookout suddenly screamed, "The chain! The chain is up!"

It was true. None could get in. But there was no turning; the tide was running in, the wind was at their backs, and the passage was a bottleneck.

Quickly the anchor dropped. Down came the sails. And the same happened with the vessel crowding behind the flagship, and with the others behind that. All came on, because there was no stopping the onrushing tide and the wind. Into the bottleneck they jammed. Spars and rigging tangled and snapped. The darkness thickened—already it was time for the *Ave María*—and the storm waxed worse.

Nobody knew what to do. The General sent men ashore to the tower that controlled the chain. The warden refused to drop the barrier.

Menéndez had anchored temporarily outside the haven. He saw what had happened, and knew the vessels had to get into port while there was still light, or they could never make it.

He ordered fifty arquebusiers into the launches and led them ashore to the walled tower. Nobody answered their shouts. Ten of his men aimed at the walls above, in case of trouble. The rest took a heavy beam and battered down the door.

They crashed through into a court, which encircled the main tower. The place was empty; the defenders were gone. But the capstan was locked in the tower, behind heavy iron doors the battering ram could not force.

While his men set to work on the iron, he sent word back

to the fleet, as a last resort telling the pilots of the flagship and the *almiranta* to hoist sail, cut the anchor cables, and hit the chain as hard as they could. Perhaps together the big galleons could break the barrier.

Menéndez saw the canvas snap out on the flagship. She moved toward the chain, picking up speed . . .

And now, with their crowbars his men burst open the iron doors. He shouldered them aside and moved quickly into the gloom of the tower. There was the capstan, and there was the chain end, held taut by a hawser around the drum. He drew his sword and struck down on the straining hemp. The strands snapped. With a thunderous rattle the chain slithered away.

They heard the cheer from the flagship as the chain fell beneath her stem. From the roof of the tower they watched as she moved swiftly into the haven, and behind her came the others.

But the danger was far from over. The tempest grew mightily. Throughout the wild night they worked to save the fleet; many cables were needed to hold the ships against the shrieking winds. The peak came at dawn. Two galleons that had anchored outside, not realizing the harbor was open, went down with four hundred people and considerable treasure. Inside, two of Mendoza's convoy and six English vessels were beached or sunk.

FAMILY ARMS OF
MENÉNDEZ DE AVILÉS

The device of the ship breaking the chain between two castles (on a red field) was granted to Ruy Pérez de Avilés, a paternal ancestor who in 1248 armed his vessels with iron-toothed prows and severed the Moorish chain defending the river at Sevilla. Ravens paired on a silver field signify the Arango family of Don Pedro's mother.
(After Ruidíaz.)

Yet their losses were trifling in comparison with what might have been. The people gave thanks to God and much credit to Don Pedro who, they asserted, was providentially endowed with the wit necessary to circumvent the devices of the devil.

And many remarked that the incident of the chain was remniscent of his ancestor, Ruy Pérez de Avilés, who with a great iron saw on the prow of his vessel, severed the Moorish chain across the River Guadalquivir and thus opened the way to capture of Sevilla in 1248. Forthwith the King had conceded to him the device of ships parting the river chain. Of course the shield of Pedro Menéndez bore this device, along with the six ravens of his mother's house.

Menéndez continued in the naval service. In 1559 at the end of the hostilities in Flanders, he brought Philip home in a stout galeass, putting him and most of his hundred and fifty chests safely ashore just ahead of a terrific storm.

As General of the King's armada, Menéndez seemed at the zenith of a brilliant career. But the royal demands on his resources — mental, physical, financial — had been too much and too long. He was tired, over-worked. Fever laid him low. Black depression hit.

To be rewarded for his service, he was to come to Toledo, Philip had said. But Toledo was far away, and promise of future reward did nothing to help the present state of a man who was sick and poor and past his fortieth birthday.

Alvaro, the well-loved elder brother, had died. Menéndez keenly felt his loss. Other kinsmen also had recently gone; and in the grip of the fever, perhaps he thought he too would die. Anyway, more than twenty months went by before he was able to travel to Toledo.

When at last he reached the court, certain ministers preceded him to the King with the rumor (which had some truth in it) that when Menéndez had the promised reward in hand he intended to retire from active service. They mentioned the great convoy to leave soon for the Indies. Its General, before his untimely death, was Alvaro Sánchez, the brother of Pedro Menéndez. Don Pedro had been ill. Now he was well. Obviously he was the one to lead the convoy.

So Philip ordered him to be the Captain General for the Fleet of the Indies. Menéndez demurred, saying that he was still not in good health and wished only to go home for a bit until he recovered, for he had seen neither his wife nor his home for a long time. Thereafter he would serve wherever the King commanded. But Philip brushed his demurral aside.

"One does not die of quartan fever," he said; and he bade Menéndez obey.

"When you return," he smiled, "you shall have your reward."

This year of 1560 was not the first time Menéndez had served as Captain General of the Fleet going to America. Six years earlier, in 1554, Philip had named him to this post against the wishes of the *Casa de Contratación* at Sevilla. The *Casa* officials were the governing body for the American trade; and they never forgave Menéndez for the royal affront to their judgment, even though Menéndez justified the King's confidence by making the trip in record time and fetching seven million pesos that were badly needed for the wars.

Captain General of the Fleet of the Indies was no empty title. This was command of the convoy which sailed from Spain to the Caribbean and back, bearing the incredible American wealth that enabled Spain to stand foremost in power among the nations of Europe.

In 1560 and again in 1561, Menéndez was Captain General. His relationships with the *Casa* did not improve, nor did he try to improve them.

One example of the friction occurred during a fleet inspection by the officers of the *Casa*. He observed that the boat standard of the inspectors was of damask crimson and bore the royal arms. This flag was only for the King — or by special privilege, for the Captain General. Menéndez quietly hauled it down and stowed it in his flag locker. The men from the *Casa* were furious.

They were dealing with a man of scrupulous honesty who believed that orders were meant to be obeyed when they were in the royal interest. Yet he did not hesitate to exceed or modify orders by the same criterion — the King's interest. Blind obedience was not in him. And this intelligent inconsistency at last gave his enemies an opening.

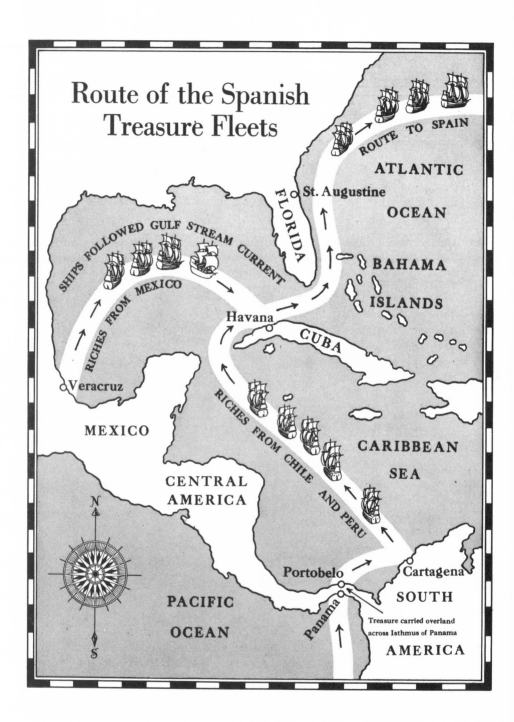

Route of the Spanish Treasure Fleets

ATLANTIC OCEAN

ROUTE TO SPAIN

FLORIDA

St. Augustine

BAHAMA

ISLANDS

SHIPS FOLLOWED GULF STREAM CURRENT

RICHES FROM MEXICO

Veracruz

Havana

CUBA

MEXICO

RICHES FROM CHILE AND PERU

CARIBBEAN

SEA

CENTRAL AMERICA

N

S

PACIFIC

OCEAN

Portobelo

Panama

Cartagena

SOUTH

Treasure carried overland across Isthmus of Panama

AMERICA

24

St. Augustine—1565

ON THEIR return from America in 1563, Menéndez and his brother Bartolomé, who was Admiral of the fleet, were thrown into prison. The *Casa* charged them with exceeding orders, breaking rules, and permissive smuggling. Martín Alonso, a family friend and sometime judge for the *Casa*, resigned his position to act as lawyer for the brothers from Avilés.

With the accused men in jail, the *Casa* saw no need to hurry with the trial.

Added to these legal troubles, heart-rending news came to Menéndez at this time. His only son had been shipwrecked near Bermuda. No one knew whether he had survived.

Menéndez petitioned the King for justice. Twice Philip ordered the *Casa* to complete the court proceedings. The prosecutors could not prove the charges. Yet the *Casa* refused to free the prisoners, and would agree only to send them to the Council of the Indies for a hearing.

First, however, the scrivener had to make copies of all the documents. By now, Menéndez had been twenty months in prison and Bartolomé twenty-five. Still the papers were not ready. It was arranged for Menéndez to break prison; and this he did, traveling by post with great secrecy to the royal palace. He entered the building about nine in the morning. As he walked down a hall, Philip saw him and sent a page to bring him to the royal bedchambers. Under the circumstances, it was illegal for an accused man to talk to the King, so Menéndez first surrendered himself to the Council for the hearing of his case.

Again there was no proof of the charges, but he was nonetheless fined a thousand ducats and Bartolomé two hundred. Philip called him at once, remitted half of the fine, and asked him to serve again as Captain General of the Fleet of the Indies.

"Everybody knows you have been accused falsely," said Philip. "Giving you the Captain General's job again will be open vindication for your insult.

"It will be like old times," he urged. "You will be General and your brothers and kinsmen will be with you."

Menéndez kissed the King's hand. "That my services have been acceptable to Your Majesty is all I can desire; and in truth I have served with full love and fidelity.

"But the King must know," he went on, "that I have a great sorrow." And he spoke of his lost son Juan, a gentleman of the royal household and General of the fleet of Mexico.

"Perhaps he and others, who have served Your Majesty for many years, still live. They may be in Florida or Bermuda. But as the King knows, I have been in prison and unable to search for them. Now by the King's leave, I would undertake to find my son."

Philip was sympathetic.

"It is my wish to help in the search for your son," he said, "if, when the search is ended, you will chart the inlets, harbors and shoals of Florida. Because this has not been done, many of our ships have been lost, and treasure and people as well. I may also mention the armadas equipped by the Emperor my father (of glorious memory) and me, for the conquest and settlement of Florida."

"Now there's a thing that really needs to be done," Menéndez said in a positive tone. "I mean the conquest and settlement of Florida. It would be in God's service as well as yours, especially in these days when so many Lutheran heretics are springing up in Flanders, Germany, France, England and Scotland.

"All those countries are near to Florida," he added (somewhat recklessly). "And Florida is a big land with such a fine climate that it surely contains a lot of good things. Yet it is peopled entirely by savages, unenlightened by Christian law. Your Majesty has an obligation to plant the Holy Gospel there.

"As for me," he went on enthusiastically, "I would take on this Florida project with greater zeal than any other you could give me!"

Philip thought of the French fort now in Florida. There was no doubt of its existence, because some of its corsairs had been captured in the Indies. It must be destroyed. The man to do it stood before him. He smiled.

"We take much pleasure," he said to Menéndez, "in committing this project to your care. We shall make a contract with you, providing everything. Within reason, of course."

So Philip gave Pedro Menéndez a new title. Henceforth he would be *Adelantado* (Leader) and Governor of Florida.

Menéndez accepted the assignment eagerly. It seemed a heaven-sent opportunity. He could search for Juan, and at the same time serve the King in the conquest of new land (as had Cortés, Pizarro, and others). He would rebuild the reputation tarnished by the *Casa*. Perhaps with luck he might even gain the fortune which thus far had eluded him.

Philip's orders were specific: *You will explore and colonize Florida; and if there be settlers or corsairs of other nations not subject to us, drive them out.*

In France, a man named Jean Ribault had orders equally specific: *Do not let Menéndez encroach upon you, any more than he would let you encroach upon him.*

Ribault's orders came from Gaspard de Coligny, Admiral of France — a France exhausted by war and torn by internal strife. Intolerance pitted Catholic against Huguenot. A few years later, the bloodletting would culminate terribly in the St. Bartholomew's Day massacre. Coligny was heartsick at the condition of his country, and strove mightily to bridge the chasm of animosities, hoping to bring Frenchmen together again in a great national purpose. What better way to unite them, than to set both Protestants and Catholics to work against a traditional enemy? The enemy, of course, was Spain.

An important part of his plan required the building of French bases in the New World. They must not be far from the wealth Spain was finding, yet not so close as to be uprooted by the first blast of Spanish anger.

So Coligny's dream became a colony planted on the St. Johns River in Florida during the summer of 1564. Most of the people were Huguenots, but they named their settlement Fort Caroline in honor of their Catholic King, teen-aged Carolus (Charles) IX.

It was not a large colony — only some three hundred; but for a while it flourished middling well. They built a three-sided fort of sod and timber, and raised palm-thatched huts, explored the country round about, and managed to antagonize a great many Indian neighbors by trying naively to make peace between warring tribes.

Their explorations amongst the natives turned up a few pounds of silver, but persistent investigators learned that it came from Spanish shipwrecks; there were no mines in Florida.

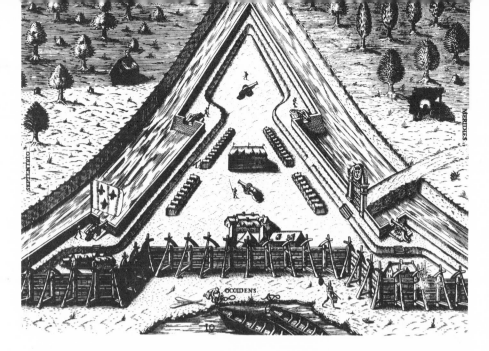

FRENCH FORT CAROLINE

The cartographer Jacques Le Moyne de Morgues sketched the fort
in 1564.   (From De Bry's *America*, 1591.)

To some of the adventurers, this discovery was too much to bear. They mutinied, seized vessels belonging to the colony, and sailed southward toward the Spanish Caribbean and the source of the silver. Within a few months, their successful pilferings by land and sea aroused the Spaniards and led to capture.

When it was learned the Frenchmen had come from a new colony in Florida, the wave of alarm reached all the way to the court of the King in Spain. Obviously the planting of this fort so close to the route of the treasure fleets was not accidental. Had not the actions of these corsairs already proved their intent?

Meanwhile, back at Fort Caroline things were not going well. The French were not farmers. They depended upon the Indians to feed them until the supply ships came. But the ships did not come; and the Indians were not so provident that they could feed the Frenchmen out of their own winter stores of corn and beans, nor so friendly as to hunt game for them.

A great flock of passenger pigeons, vulnerable even to inept hunters, saved the colony from starvation; but a year in the wilderness was enough of adventure. Surely, France had forgotten them.

So they shouted for joy when John Hawkins, the English slave trader, happened into the river to fill his water casks; and Hawkins was persuaded to give one of his four ships in exchange for cannon and gunpowder, for which he thought he might find good use in the future.

By August 15, 1565, the colonists were ready to sail for France. But summer winds in Florida are easterly, making it hard to work out of the river. Impatiently they waited for the wind to change.

France had not forgotten. Already a fleet was on the way to Fort Caroline. It was captained by Jean Ribault, a man of unusual experience and ability. He came with desperate urgency, knowing that Pedro Menéndez was also on the way.

Menéndez sailed from Cádiz in June. His armada numbered ten vessels, and coming from the north country were many others, ships and people led by his friends and relatives. Altogether, over thirty vessels were bound for Florida with some twenty-six hundred people. Most were military men, for the first task was to join battle with the French; but there were also administrators, priests, farmers and artisans -- millers, tanners, locksmiths, silversmiths (they thought precious metal was sure to be found), and others. Many families were along.

The crossing was stormy. The fleet was scattered, but there was a rendezvous of sorts at Puerto Rico, and Menéndez decided to push ahead of the stragglers. Ribault's fleet was nearing Florida, and delay now would be fatal because each day would better the French position.

The Spaniards left Puerto Rico August 15, five ships and six hundred people. Hoping to forge ahead of Ribault within the thousand long miles to Florida, they sailed a short cut, north through the Bahamas, directly for Florida. It was an untried route, and dangerous.

One night the flagship *San Pelayo* struck three times, but a quartering sea carried her off the bank. Another night they saw a comet born in the sky over their heads. Bright as a sun it streaked toward Florida. A good omen it was; the next morning they found themselves in the deep water of the Bahama Channel.

But they did not overtake the French.

Jean Ribault won the race to Florida. On August 28 he sailed quietly up the St. Johns, giving the colonists at Fort Caroline some uneasy moments until across the water they recognized his great red beard. Then up went the shout of welcome!

Now they were more than seven hundred strong. Suddenly there was no more talk of going back to France.

The very same day, August 28, which is the feast day of Saint Augustine, the good Bishop of Hippo, the little Spanish armada made the Florida landfall.

They saw the white beaches of Cape Cañaveral (today called Kennedy), then sailed northward along the coast, looking for the French. On they went, sailing by day and anchoring by night. There were calms and headwinds; and suspense and uncertainty increased as they saw no signs of life along the low-lying, featureless shore. At last, while they lay at anchor the fourth night, fires flickered in the distant woodland. Menéndez resolved to land a scouting party.

The next morning, September 2, Fieldmaster Valdés took twenty soldiers and went ashore.

Indians, armed with bows and arrows, were waiting. Their hair was in a top-knot and they wore little else except deerskin loincloths and earrings made of inflated fish bladders, which shone in the sun like pearls. Intricate tattooing covered much of their bodies.

They were members of the Timucua nation, which at this period lived in the region centered on the St. Johns River. Being fishermen and hunters as well as farmers, they were not strangers to the coast. Neither did they seem strangers to white men. By means of signs they told Valdés the French were farther to the north.

The next morning Menéndez himself came ashore to meet the natives before resuming the search. "They seem to be a noble race," he wrote Philip, reporting on this first contact.

Eight leagues farther north the Spaniards reached "a good harbor with a good beach" (in the words of the old narrative), "to which the *Adelantado* gave the name of *San Agustín*." The day was probably September 3.

Again they coasted north, and about two o'clock on the afternoon of September 4 they sighted four large galleons at anchor off the mouth of a great river. The French at last!

But a squall hit while they were still half a league distant. And the rain stole the wind. Not until after dusk did the breeze come back. Then the sky cleared swiftly into serene night, and the five Spanish ships pushed on.

At half past eleven, warning shots from the French cannon whistled through their rigging. Fortunately there was no damage. Menéndez sent his men below for safety and kept his own artillery silent.

The French galleons were anchored close together, their prows pointing toward land, as if sniffing a trace of the forest in the land breeze. Menéndez planned to anchor to the windward. Then he would pay out the cables until his vessels were abreast of the enemy. At dawn's light they would grapple and board, before help came from the fort.

The first part of the plan was beautifully executed. The armada came steadily on, without regard for the French cannon. One after another, the anchors dropped. The hooks gripped bottom, and each ship came to a restless halt at the end of her cable.

Skilfully Menéndez put his *San Pelayo* between the bows of two Frenchmen — Ribault's big flagship *Trinity,* and the Admiral's galleon. In the darkness it seemed to those aboard that the French prows were like giant pikes ready to impale them. The *Trinity's* mainmast bore the standard and a royal ensign. The other galleon flaunted the Admiral's flag at her foremast. The banners lifted proudly in the night wind. There was no sound except the surge of the water and the creak of the rigging.

Menéndez bade the trumpets hail the *Trinity* (though the vessels were not eight fathoms apart). The French returned the salute.

In courteous French he called to them: "Messieurs, where does your armada come from?"

"From France," a voice told him.

"Why is it here?"

"We bring infantry, artillery and supplies for the King's fort," was the reply.

In response to the next question, they informed him they were of the "new religion." Jean Ribault was their leader. And who are you, they asked.

"I am Pedro Menéndez de Avilés," he shouted. Now he dropped all pretense at diplomacy.

"I am General of this armada of the King of Spain. I come to hang all the heretics I find here. These are my orders from the King. I carry them out at dawn as I board your ships."

His words struck them like a blow. The shocked silence ended with an angry, cursing roar from the men lining the rail

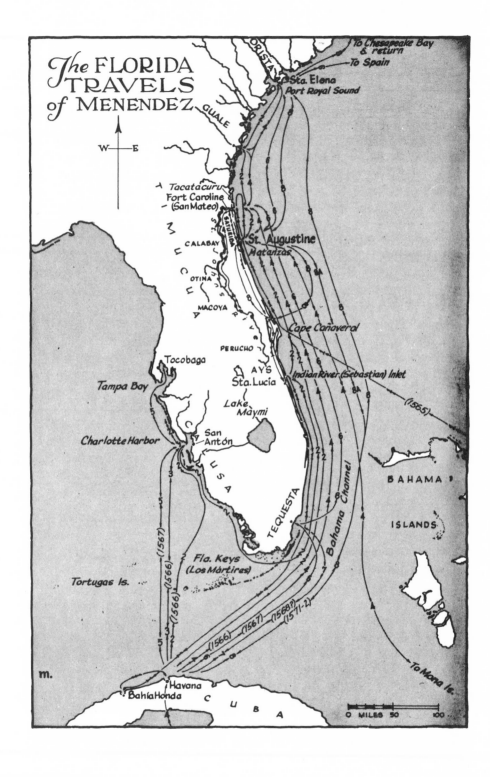

The FLORIDA TRAVELS of MENENDEZ

W—E

To Chesapeake Bay & return
To Spain
Sta. Elena
Port Royal Sound

ORISTA

GUALE

Tacatacuru
Fort Caroline
(San Mateo)

SATURIBA

CALABAY

St. Augustine
Matanzas

OTINA

MACOYA

Cape Cañaveral

PERUCHO

Indian River (Sebastian) Inlet

AYS
Sta. Lucía

Tocobaga

Lake
Màymi

Tampa Bay

(1565)

San
Antón

Charlotte Harbor

BAHAMA

ISLANDS

TEQUESTA

Bahama Channel

(1567)

(1566)

Fla. Keys
(Los Màrtires)

Tortugas Is.

(1566)

(1566)

(1567)

(1568?)

(1571-2)

m.

To Mona Is.

Havana
Bahía Honda

CUBA

0 MILES 50 100

of the *Trinity*. The epithets were directed principally against King Philip and his man Menéndez, and the gist of it was "that's for King Philip and this is for Menéndez, and if you've got any guts you'll fight right now!"

These were words to burn any man's ears. The plan to wait for daylight was forgotten.

"Pay out the cable!" roared Menéndez. "Board the enemy!"

Then, as the sailors were slow at the capstan, he leaped from the poop and ran forward to take charge. The cable was too many turns around the drum; it had to be unwound before it would go free.

On the *Trinity*, the French heard the shouted command and saw his fury as he charged to the capstan. With their own soldiers ashore, they had no wish for combat. Forthwith they cut the cable, spread sail, and fled. The three other Frenchmen did the same.

Seeing the quarry about to slip out of his grasp, Menéndez gave orders to cut cables and pursue. The gunners got off five shots, but in the darkness it was impossible to tell whether there were any hits. The French quartet suddenly divided, two heading north and two going south.

Menéndez sent three of his vessels on the southern chase, instructing them to rendezvous with him in the morning. The *San Pelayo* and the *patache* took after the northbound galleons.

It was clear that the French would not risk a fight, lightly manned as they were. They soon outdistanced the storm-damaged Spanish vessels. At dawn, Menéndez gave the order to turn back, and by ten in the morning was off St. Johns bar again.

They went inshore far enough to count five French craft anchored in the river. On the beach were two companies of soldiers, each with its colors. A cannon flashed and smoked. Menéndez made sail for the harbor of St. Augustine.

There on Thursday, September 6, he was joined by the others, who had also returned empty-handed. The anchorage was in deep water outside the port, for neither the *San Pelayo* nor the *San Salvador* could cross the shallow bar.

At once he began putting his men ashore. Among the first to go were Captains Andrés López Patiño and Juan de San Vicente, who would choose a place to build a fort. As the landing boats made the bar and entered the blue-green waters of the little bay, the men could see dark-skinned natives on the land, their huts half hidden in the forest behind them.

33

The Indians greeted them in friendship, and soon escorted the captains to a large building of posts and poles, thatched with palm. This was the communal house of the village of Seloy.

The dusky interior, blackened with the memory of a thousand hearthfires and laden with the smell of human use, seemed a strange haven after the bright sea air. But before the talk was through, the Cacique had given the Spaniards leave to make this building their fort. At once they set about making it defensible by digging a moat around it and piling the earth into a parapet. This they did "with only their fingernails," says the record, for the entrenching tools were still aboard a ship that had not arrived.

On Friday, the three smaller ships came over the bar and landed three hundred more people, including the women and children. Twenty bronze guns were set ashore.

September 8 was Saturday. The last hundred people were landed.

In mid-afternoon, the entire colony gathered near the landing, for Menéndez was coming ashore. There were five hundred soldiers, in addition to the hundred "useless people" (as Menéndez termed them) — family men, women, children and officials.

Since eight o'clock this morning, two French ships had hovered offshore, threatening the *San Pelayo* and the *San Salvador*. Menéndez held his galleons as they were, and signaled the Frenchmen to approach. But they were wary. They came within half a league of the *San Pelayo*, and even peered into the harbor. Then, as the westering sun shot quicksilver darts into their eyes from the swift shore-bound waves, they sailed north to tell Ribault what they had seen.

With mixed feelings, Menéndez watched them go. They would be back, and others with them. He dropped into the launch for the trip ashore.

It was after three when the boat made the harbor. Ahead, the soldiers were mustered near the landing, and close by were the officials and the colonists with their women and children. The Indians were also on hand, gravely watching the Spaniards and inspecting goods and supplies with much curiosity.

Pedro Menéndez de Avilés, *Adelantado* and Governor and General of King Philip's forces in Florida, stepped ashore amidst the sound of trumpet and drum, the firing of cannon, and the shouts of the six hundred. The banners of Spain made a brave sight as he set foot on Florida soil.

THE FOUNDING OF ST. AUGUSTINE
(Courtesy of Frederic Ray.)

35

Father López, the Chaplain, was already ashore. He came forward with the cross, singing the *Te Deum Laudamus*. Menéndez walked directly to the cross and kneeled to touch it with his lips. And so did all who came with him; and likewise the Indians, who had observed with great interest.

The Father offered a solemn Mass. When it was ended, Menéndez proclaimed possession of the land in the name of the Crown. Next he administered the oath of loyalty to those who would serve as the King's officials and as military officers.

And thus was St. Augustine founded, with pomp and proclamation, solemnity and promise of fidelity, amid the martial sounds of music and artillery and the happy clamor of people who, after a long voyage, have at last found home.

As should all important occasions, this one ended with food for everybody. Afterwards, Menéndez inspected the new fort. What he saw surprised and pleased him, and he warmly complimented Patiño, who had kept the work going all night so that today it would be a true defense.

He called the captains into council. It was decided they would unload all the supplies they could within the next three days, then send the two galleons back to Santo Domingo. Since these big vessels could not get into the harbor, they were in constant danger of capture, if indeed a storm did not beach them first.

The *San Pelayo* weighed anchor at midnight September 10, and the *San Salvador* soon after. Menéndez waved them off from the *San Pelayo's* launch, a good-sized craft normally towed from the galleon's stern. Then, accompanied also by a *patache*, he headed through the gloom for the harbor. The two craft were deeply laden with supplies and ordnance and a hundred and fifty soldier-stevedores.

Half a league from the bar, the wind failed. There was nothing to do but anchor and wait. They spent the night buttoned against the chill salt damp, their cramped bodies complaining of the hard decks and the incessant pitch and roll.

But dawn came at last, and with it a shout that galvanized the weary men. Looming to the seaward were the spars of two French galleons!

The overloaded Spanish boats drew too much water to cross the bar until the tide rose, hours from now. The soldiers were unarmed; to make more room for supplies, they had left their weapons ashore. There was no wind. The defenseless cargoes were a prize plum for the French, and easily plucked. For the great ships came on slowly, their high topsails gathering air that did not touch the sea surface, nor the Spanish sails.

The Spaniards could do nothing — except pray. Their prayers, it is said, were directed to Our Lady of Utrera, asking her for the favor of a little wind. And the ripples came upon the water! The boats gathered way.

But the French came even faster, and so close that someone — perhaps Ribault himself — hailed the Spaniards to surrender, saying they would come to no harm. Menéndez did not answer. His eyes were on the breakers that marked the apron of the bar.

Tide had turned and the breeze held. The vessels nosed toward port. Beneath their stems, the water shoaled fast. But they did not strike. In a few moments they were in the deeper, calmer water of the harbor. Menéndez looked back to see the big galleons, dangerously close to the shallows, turn away fast. *A good thing the* San Pelayo *has a few hours start,* he thought.

And in the clear morning light, farther out to sea, were four other vessels. Indeed Ribault had come in force. His plan, as Menéndez had foreseen, was to capture the two crippled galleons. But the galleons were gone, and now even the two lesser prizes had slipped through his fingers. Ashore, the Spaniards were obviously well entrenched on the far side of the harbor, well beyond the reach of attackers who might land on the coast.

Ribault decided to go after the missing galleons. Surely his own vessels could catch the broken-masted *San Pelayo,* and her loss would badly cripple the new-born colony.

But the air that had pushed Menéndez safely into the haven also swelled the sails of the *San Pelayo* and the *San Salvador.* Then the weather, fair up to now, made a change. The wind began pressing from the northeast and the sea rose high. Driven before the mounting gale, the French went flying south, desperately striving to haul into the wind and away from the thundering surf.

Victory over the French

A S THE storm continued, Menéndez' uncanny weather sense told him this was no summer squall, but a great equinoctial disturbance that would batter the coast for several days. Even if the French weathered it, they could not possibly get back to Fort Caroline within a week.

He called a council. Raising his voice above the rush of the wind and the rattle of the rain on the palm thatch, he convinced his captains they should march overland and capture Fort Caroline while Ribault and most of its defenders were gone.

The sound of trumpet, fife and drum woke St. Augustine at dawn on September 16, a Sunday. Father López had the church bells sounded, and all came to Mass. At its end, the sergeants formed up the five hundred — for each captain, fifty men. A third were pikemen. The rest carried the heavy arquebuses, except for twenty axemen — Basques and Asturians from the wooded mountains of north Spain — who were the vanguard. Every man packed his own weapons and carried eight days' rations of biscuit in his rucksack.

Menéndez led out with the axemen. Martín Ochoa, a Basque, was their captain. Two Indian brothers had appeared providentially as guides. The French prisoner Jean Francois was along. (He was one of those who had left Fort Caroline and turned corsair, only to be captured in the Caribbean and turned over to Menéndez.)

The axemen moved fast, clearing and blazing the trail. The main force followed at a less strenuous pace under Valdés, the Fieldmaster, and Sergeant-major Villaroel.

The sun came out for a little while and seemed to set the whole world steaming with its heat. Perhaps the brief clear spell was the eye of the great storm, for soon the wind and rain came again with new force. Days of high tides and rain torrents had flooded the land. The "trail" the Indians followed was knee deep in water. Streams that had to be crossed were swollen into rivers.

At the first crossing, Menéndez seized a soldier's pike and waded forward. When he got to the deep water, he used the long pikestaff as a float and swam across. Others did the same. Men who could not swim clung to the pikes and were ferried across by the swimmers.

He called a halt as they reached ground above the flood. When the last straggler had arrived, again he set out with the axemen. Valdés let the troop rest a few more minutes before he gave the order to follow.

And so it went. March and rest, march and rest, until dark. Their camp that night had little comfort, but the men were too tired to care.

The second day was like the first — the flood underfoot and the downpours above. The wind lashed the forest. Great limbs, torn from the trees, crashed down to block the passage. Branches thrashed wildly, and the vines that laced the underbrush jerked and danced and laid hold of the pikes like true friends of the enemy.

The third day was no better; nor was the fourth. Everything was soaked, clothing, food, gunpowder and matchcords. The arquebuses were useless. But at last they were coming close to the target.

At sunset the rain stopped for a time. Menéndez led his men to a stand of pine where there was little chance of discovery by enemy scouts. This night the stragglers were very slow to come in. It was past ten before the last bone-weary arquebusier dragged in. The bivouac was completely cheerless. The vale of the pines had become a vast pond. Some of the men stood in water to their hips. The trees moaned in the wind. The rain started again.

Yet some of the men still had the stamina to grumble. A few openly showed insolence.

"We've been sold out by that Asturian grape-treader," a voice said loudly. "A jackass knows more about fighting than he does!"

Menéndez pretended not to hear. This was no time for discipline.

Two hours before dawn he brought his officers into council. He talked and he listened, and then he talked again; and at last all agreed to continue on to the fort, despite their desperate condition.

He ordered them to their knees. "Pray," he said. "Pray — for victory."

As he gave the command to march, Menéndez took the lead, with the French prisoner as the guide. A rope bound Francois' hands behind him and Menéndez himself held the end of it.

In the greyness of dawn Francois picked up the trail and they set out, the whole troop under strict orders to follow at once. The Frenchman turned to Menéndez.

"The fort is beyond the hill," he said, "washed by the water of the river."

Francois was right. The fort was there. And inside, the sentinels lay abed. All night they had been vigilant; but as daylight approached, their captain looked at the downpour and sent the sodden men to their quarters. *Sacre bleu! Warfare in such weather is impossible.* He walked back to his own room . . .

Menéndez sent Valdés and Ochoa to scout the fort. They slipped swiftly over the hill and onto the plain below. The rain muffled any sound they made. They could see the huts of the settlement, and beyond, the low fort. It was a three-sided defense with bastions; and the land walls, as well as they could make out, were moated earthworks crowned by a sod parapet.

They saw no one; but not wanting to risk a closer approach, they turned back, only to find a stranger in front of them.

"Who goes there?" came the call in French.

In the same language the Basque answered, "Frenchmen." He kept walking, and the other came on to meet him.

A few steps away the Frenchman stopped, uncertain, and half drew his sword. The Basque rushed him and struck at his face with sheathed sword. The Frenchman warded off the blow. Valdés came up with buckler and sword ready. He lunged at the Frenchman, who fell clumsily to the ground, shouting the alarm.

Pedro Menéndez heard the shouts and came to an instant decision. He looked at his captains — Recalde, Amaya, Patiño — good men all, and their men behind them.

"Santiago!" he roared the battle cry. "At the enemy! God's help! Victory! Valdés has taken the fort!"

Their General's voice sent them pelting down the path toward the fort. There was no thought of marching order — only lightening joy at the incredible news and the fierce surge of excitement that drove them on to share in the victory.

Through the rain, Valdés saw them coming. He thrust his sword into the Frenchman, and with a cry of triumph turned and ran with his men toward Fort Caroline.

The confusion of pounding footsteps and hoarse shouts from the onrushing horde brought settlers to the doors of their huts. The cries of warning became frantic, desperate. Someone at the fort recognized the sound of the terror outside and opened the wicket of the main gate for the refugees. Valdés was there, to slip inside and kill the gateman. And after him came many of his comrades.

A French trumpeter had just mounted the rampart to see what was disturbing the countryside when the Spaniards burst into the fort. His trumpet blared the alarm. Out of their quarters came the defenders, a few ready for battle, but most of them naked or in their shirts and undone by surprise.

René de Laudonnière, their leader, tried to rally them. A few responded, and bravely they engaged the Spaniards at a wall breach.

Moments later, Laudonnière stood almost alone, gripping his sword and buckler. At Menéndez' shoulder, Francois saw him and shouted, "There stands their leader!"

A Spanish trumpet sounded victory. The long pikes forced Laudonnière back. He turned and fled into his house, the pikemen hot after him.

But the fighting was almost over. Now the Spaniards were searching out those hidden in the houses. Menéndez shouted an order to spare the women and children.

Laudonnière escaped. So did the artist Jacques LeMoyne, and many others. But of two hundred and forty in the garrison, a hundred and thirty-two were dead. The victory was won. And let none who remember the incredible march through the storm say it was unearned.

At noon Menéndez took off his clothing and found a bed, where he ate his meal and rested. By four o'clock he was up and dressed to meet with the captains. Since tomorrow, September 21, was St. Matthew's Day, the fort would be called San Mateo, he explained. Villaroel was sworn in as its commander. He and Valdés began checking the rolls to pick three hundred soldiers for the garrison.

Roll call confirmed the suspicion that only four hundred troops had reached the fort. Some had lost heart and turned back, saying they had missed the trail; others had simply given out from exhaustion.

With thirty-five picked men, Menéndez set out for St. Augustine early on September 22. For if Jean Ribault had somehow survived the storm, he might even now be at St. Augustine.

Much of the way was worse than before. The water had risen even higher. But at last on the third day they neared the settlement. One of the younger soldiers jogged ahead with the news. His shouts brought Father López running to hear the welcome cry: "Victory! The French fort is ours!"

Trembling with excitement, the Chaplain hurried to his house and put on his best cassock and surplice. Carrying the crucifix, he went out to meet the returning soldiers.

And there in the trail, as they saw the priest coming, Menéndez and his men fell to their knees and gave thanks. Then Father López and those who had come with him turned and led the troop into St. Augustine, singing the *Te Deum*. In the tumultuous rejoicing of their friends, the heroes forgot their weariness.

A few days after his return from San Mateo (erstwhile Fort Caroline), Menéndez learned from the Indians that many white men were coming toward St. Augustine from the south. For the moment, they were halted at a deep inlet four leagues away. He knew these were survivors from Ribault's fleet. So it had been wrecked in the storm!

With fifty men, he left St. Augustine. That night they bivouacked at the south end of Anastasia Island. Across the inlet they could see the campfires of the enemy.

At daybreak Menéndez kept his men out of sight behind the sand dunes. The French were up early, foraging along the shore for shellfish as men whose bellies had been empty a long time. Before long, one appeared with a flag. He tied it to a staff planted on the beach.

All this Menéndez had observed. *Perhaps hunger has taken the fight out of them,* he thought. To find out, he changed his gentleman's clothing for sailor's garb and, accompanied by one of his French prisoners, he walked out onto the beach in full view of the men on the opposite shore. He shouted to make sure they saw him.

The French gathered quickly at the water's edge. The inlet here was perhaps only fifty fathoms wide, but the clear green water raced through the channel so swiftly that only a strong swimmer could hope to get across. Now such a one was leaving his companions, and soon he stood panting before Menéndez.

Arrangements were made for a parley, and the French captain and his aides were ferried across in a supply boat. The spokesman soon came to the point.

"Be so kind," he said, "as to lend us the boat to cross this arm of the sea. We wish to go to our fort twenty leagues from here."

"Gentlemen," said Menéndez, "we have taken your fort and killed all the people in it except the women and children."

And seeing their looks of unbelief, he went on: "Sit down and eat. I will send you two prisoners and trophies from the fort."

While the French were breakfasting and talking to their captured countrymen and looking at the trophies, Menéndez went to eat with his own men. The French were allotted an hour to swallow the food and try to digest the facts. Then Menéndez confronted them again.

"If you want to surrender your arms and put yourselves at my mercy, I will treat you as God directs me. Do as you please, but I will make no other truce with you."

After much time and many words, the spokesman brought the flags and weapons of France to Menéndez.

"We are at your mercy," he said.

Twenty soldiers manned the boat and brought the French across the inlet ten at a time. Each group was given food and drink before the next ten arrived. And after the first ten had eaten, their hands were tied behind them with matchcords from the arquebuses. So it was done with each ten, until more than two hundred men were bound.

Ten of the prisoners were Catholics. They were put aboard the boat sailing for St. Augustine. The rest made ready to march by land.

Menéndez instructed his captains. Then, carrying a short lance, he walked ahead toward St. Augustine. This was Saturday, September 29, the Day of Saint Michael, prince of the Church militant. It had been another miraculous day; fifty men had captured two hundred. He stopped for a moment at a level stretch, as though admiring the view to the west, where the sky promised a glorious sunset. With the point of the lance, he marked a line in the sand before he went on.

A few minutes later the others came, herding the prisoners. The captain in the lead saw the line marked across the trail and gave the order for the execution. The dry sand seemed

43

SURRENDER AT MATANZAS

(Courtesy of Frederic Ray.)

thirsty for the blood of the bound men, and the noise of death was soon over.

In the dusk the Spaniards again took the trail. They reached St. Augustine at dawn.

It is remarkable that the macabre act was repeated on October 12, when Menéndez met Ribault and another band of castaways at the same inlet. The parley took place as before. Ribault saw the cadavers that still lay amidst the sand dunes. He spoke to captives who verified the loss of Fort Caroline. To Menéndez he said:

"What has happened to me could also happen to you. Since our Kings are brothers in marriage and friends, you should treat me as a friend. Let me have ships and supplies to return to France."

Perhaps Menéndez remembered the heart-stopping sight of Ribault's galleons in the dawn off St. Augustine. He would agree to nothing except unconditional surrender, although Ribault and a hundred and fifty of his men offered a hundred thousand ducats for their lives.

They too were brought ten by ten, and tied and slain, except for the musicians, and four others who claimed to be Catholics.

From this time, the inlet was called *Matanzas* — the Place of •Slaughters.

That night Menéndez was back in St. Augustine, and the people were relieved to know their leader had won again. Ribault would threaten them no more; his head now decorated a pikestaff. True, some thought Menéndez was cruel. But most, being practical about the matter, rated him a good captain. There was not enough food for both Frenchmen and Spaniards. Besides, the prisoners outnumbered their captors. Furthermore, since the French were heretics, it was legally permissible to burn them; instead, Menéndez had granted them honorable death with blades of steel.

Menéndez himself, having made the necessary decision, wasted no time in justifying it. A few days later, he wrote King Philip a report: "I had Jean Ribault and all the rest put to the knife, as was necessary for God's service and yours."

Ribault is dead, he thought. *I can be generous now.* So he wrote:

"It is most fortunate that Ribault is dead, because the King of France could do more with him and fifty thousand ducats than with others and ten times fifty thousand. This man **did** more in one year than another in ten. He was the most experienced seaman and corsair known."

Ribault could have asked for no better epitaph!

The only dangerous French group still in Florida were those who had refused to surrender with Ribault, and had fled from Matanzas. News of their doings soon reached St. Augustine. They had gone many leagues along the beach to the south, where the *Trinity* had been wrecked. Here they were building a fort and a ship. Putting an end to the French affair, Menéndez decided, could be combined with a reconnaissance of the south and an urgent trip to Havana for provisions.

They left St. Augustine on November 2, reinforced by a detachment from San Mateo. With Indian guides, Menéndez led a hundred and fifty men by land. Diego Amaya went by sea with three vessels, carrying the arms and supplies and another hundred soldiers. The weather was good, and the two forces paralleled each other down the coast. Marching light, the soldiers made good time on the firm, wide beaches. They would start at two in the morning and walk until daylight, rest two hours, walk until about eleven, rest two more hours, and then walk until sunset. In this way they covered about twenty-five miles a day. The boats kept the same pace and anchored offshore each night opposite the campfires.

In the grey dawn of November 26, the guides brought them to the place where the French were, not far from the battered hulk of the *Trinity*. Nervous sentries had already seen their land-and-sea approach, and when they reached the fort, the French were gone.

Carefully they entered the gate, guarding against surprise, half expecting a trick. For with its six cannon and plenty of gunpowder, the crude wooden fort looked quite capable of mounting a defense. Inside, they found food, also from the *Trinity;* and at this the Spaniards were in high good humor, because they had been on half rations ever since leaving St. Augustine.

Menéndez called one of the French musicians, a trumpeter taken at Matanzas, and sent him into the woods to proclaim that the ones who surrendered would live. The fellow soon found the refugees.

"Rather than surrender to the Spaniards I prefer to be devoured by the Indians," said the French captain bitterly, and turned away. A few followed him. But most, tired and discouraged, were ready to give up. With a last look at the men they would never see again, they walked behind the trumpeter onto the beach and laid down their arms.

Menéndez received them cheerfully and generously. The nobles among them were brought to dine with him, and their tattered clothing was replaced from his own stores. The others were provided for among his men.

That afternoon they continued down the coast. On the second day they reached Indian River Inlet and the village of the Cacique called Ays. They were welcomed, and Ays helped them choose a promising camp site where the cabbage palms and coco-plums grew, and fishing was good.

Then, having provided for his men as best he could, Menéndez took fifty soldiers and half of the French prisoners aboard the two *pataches* and set out for Havana. A storm almost foundered them, but at last they reached the port and were overjoyed to find there three vessels of the Asturian fleet, left behind in the ocean crossing.

Later, Menéndez went to Governor Osorio, armed with the royal decrees which commanded the governor to aid the conquest and settlement of Florida. Osorio refused, however, to honor the King's instructions, saying there was no money. Menéndez had to look elsewhere.

On the way to Havana, the Asturians had captured a Portuguese prize. It was now sold to buy provisions, which were promptly loaded aboard the two *pataches* and sent to Florida. The emergency of the moment was relieved, and Menéndez then took the little Asturian armada and set out for Hispaniola. This island was a favorite wintering place for corsairs laden with plunder after a summer's work in the Caribbean. With good fortune, two or three more prizes might be captured here and sold to help the Florida project.

A dispatch boat brought news that changed their plans. Eighteen hundred men would come to Florida in March, and Menéndez must procure the meat and fish to feed them for the next nine months. The corsair hunt was abandoned. Vessels went to Yucatan and Hispaniola for supplies.

Early in January of 1566 Esteban de las Alas showed up with another duo of Asturian vessels, accompanied by two ships from Santo Domingo. Menéndez had all of them careened and readied for the work to come.

Meanwhile, disquieting word arrived from Florida. A hundred of the people at St. Augustine had died. Of the survivors, many were ready to abandon Florida at the first chance.

Menéndez was alarmed. The project could be wrecked very speedily if some of these disgruntled ones were allowed forth to boast of their frontier hardships. Immigration would stop. And the fortune he had already put into the venture would be lost. Once again he wrote Philip. This time it was to ask the King to punish deserters from Florida by sending them to the galleys — in Florida.

Clearly a strong hand was needed in the colony. But before returning north, Menéndez wanted to explore the Keys and the southwestern coast where, it was said, many Spanish castaways had been enslaved by the Indians. Perhaps, too, he was still hoping for word of his own lost son.

The Unwelcome Wife

ON FEBRUARY 10, 1566, they left Havana with seven vessels and five hundred men. The plan was to discover a safe passage between the Tortugas Islands and the Mártires (Florida Keys) for the fleets sailing the Gulf current from Veracruz to Havana. Then they would continue on to Florida's southwest coast, searching for good harbors and a site for the fort Menéndez wanted to build near the imagined southwestern mouth of the St. Johns River. In the course of the exploration, they hoped to rescue the shipwrecked men and women. These tasks done, they would set the course for St. Augustine, then go north to make further settlements, if possible.

The first part of the plan was successfully completed with the discovery of the deep water east of Tortugas. Afterward they sighted the low-lying Florida coast.

On the fourth day, Amaya was in the lead by half a league when a canoe put out from the nearby shore. In it was one man, naked except for a breechclout and the paint on his skin. But the shout he gave them, as he came closer, was in Spanish!

With his guidance, Menéndez took a pair of small sailing galleys (*bergantines*) into the bay called Charlotte Harbor, and anchored them prow to stern along a deep shore.

The castaway said that most of his brother captives were in the town of the cacique named Carlos, half a league away. But there were only a few survivors — perhaps a dozen — of the two hundred or more people shipwrecked on these coasts. All the rest had been sacrificed to the devil by Carlos or his father before him.

On hearing this, Menéndez sent him to invite Carlos to visit the *bergantines;* and the next morning the chieftain came, escorted along the trail by three hundred of his archers. He proceeded to a seat on the platform Menéndez had provided at the water's edge near the vessels. Menéndez left his craft and went to meet him. Thirty arquebusiers, their matches lit, also disembarked.

Carlos was a handsome young man of about twenty-five years. As Menéndez sat near him, Carlos knelt, with the palms of his hands turned upward, and Menéndez joined hands with him in this gesture of respect and friendship. Then came the gifts: a bar of silver for Menéndez; and for Carlos a shirt, silk breeches, a doublet and a hat. The Indian donned them at once, and with his proud youthful demeanor looked very much the gentleman. Other gifts were presented to the principal Indians, and there were also things to be taken to Carlos' wives.

Carlos could not resist an invitation to come aboard, and twenty of his men followed. They were a little disturbed when the lines were loosed and the vessels headed for open water; but the interpreter quieted them, explaining that the move was merely a precaution to keep the *bergantines* from being upset by too many visitors.

The Spanish hospitality — the unfamiliar food and the strange clothing he had received — greatly pleased Carlos; but since all good things must come to an end, at last he signified that he was ready to leave.

At this point, it was suddenly clear to each native guest that a Spaniard stood by his side, and grim-faced soldiers lined the rails so that no man might leap overboard and swim to freedom. Carlos kept his seat. The interpreter began to speak:

"The King of Spain has sent us for the Christian men and women you hold captive. You will bring them to us, or you will die. Deliver them, and you shall be rewarded."

"Very good," replied Carlos, after slight reflection. "I shall myself go for them at once."

And he started to rise, but a glance at the face of Menéndez changed his mind.

"Tell him," said Menéndez, "that my men will kill him if he moves. Let him send one or two of his men."

Carlos obeyed with alacrity, and the *bergantines* headed back toward the landing. Within the hour, eight of the white slaves — five women and three men — were tearfully and noisily greeting their countrymen. The Indians, laden with gifts and expressions of friendship, were now free to go.

A few days later, after a fruitless search for other survivors farther north, Menéndez returned to the same anchorage; and at the cacique's urging, arranged to pay a visit to the Indian town the next morning.

He did not go alone. The entourage included an ensign with the banner, nine instrumentalists (two each of fifers, drummers and trumpeters; and psalterist, harpist and fiddler), a dwarf who sang and danced — and two hundred arquebusiers. They were able to land fairly close to the town, and paraded to the great house of the cacique, where the reception was to take place.

According to the chronicle, this palm-thatched house was so big that it held two thousand people without crowding. Large windows ventilated one side, and seated on the ground outside these windows were several hundred young girls. Menéndez, after noting the windows, halted his arquebusiers in a place where they could see what went on inside the building. The matches for their weapons were kept burning.

He went to the doorway, followed by twenty of his gentlemen. They estimated that a thousand Indians were squatted on the earth floor, men on one side, women on the other. On a dais near the center sat two figures, proudly erect and clearly in authority. One was Carlos. The other was a woman, whom the Spaniards took to be the principal wife of the young cacique.

Slowly they approached the dais. Carlos made a sign that Menéndez should mount the platform. He yielded his own seat and made as if to sit apart. But Menéndez insisted that they remain side by side, whereupon Carlos arose and took Menéndez' hands upon his own.

The woman on the dais came to do the same. As she did so, the Indian girls outside the windows began to sing in chorus, and continued without pause. The girls, between ten and fifteen years old, were seated in groups. Half the groups would sing for a while, then the other half would take up the song. Other Indians danced and whirled about in time with the music.

After awhile the dancing ended (though the chorus kept on singing), and Carlos suggested having something to eat. But Menéndez, in the best of humor, informed him it was much too early to eat.

Now Menéndez, who had an ear for speech as well as music, had provided himself with a written list of polite words and phrases in the native tongue. Fancying himself somewhat of a ladies' man, he wished to present gifts to Carlos' wife and sister, without using the interpreter to do so.

Turning to the woman on the dais, he spoke in her own language the speech composed for the edification of the cacique's

THE NEW WORLD OF MENÉNDEZ
(Shaded area indicates territory controlled by Spain)

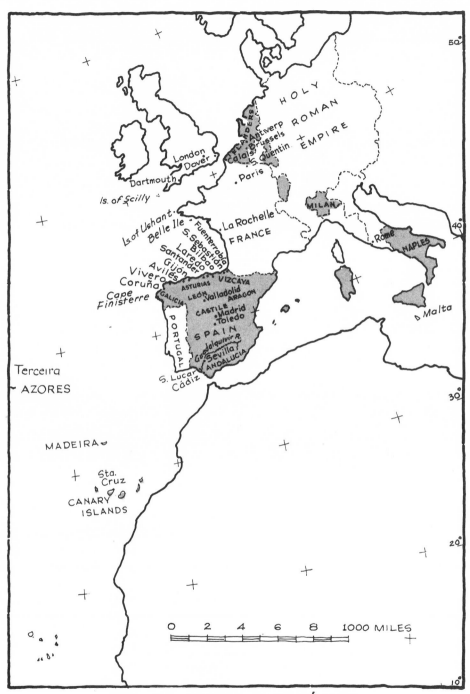

THE OLD WORLD OF MENÉNDEZ
(Shaded area indicates land ruled by Spain)

53

wife. The Indians, at first amazed, began to show amusement. The lady lowered her eyes as befitted modesty. Menéndez was quite pleased with the effect of his little conceit, until the interpreter blurted out:

"She's not his wife, but his sister — the one he has given *you* for a wife."

Momentarily chagrined, Menéndez quickly recovered. He rose and took his bride-to-be by the hand, and led her to a seat between Carlos and himself. Then with a smile he began all over again, this time using the proper speech. Many little things he said to her, reading as need be from his paper; and the whole assemblage was mightily pleased. So too, perhaps, was the bride, although she had little to say. Indeed, she was a quiet one, in her thirties and rather plain, though her dignity as a princess was becoming.

In order to use his other speech, Menéndez asked Carlos to send for his principal wife. The entrance of this young woman (she was about twenty) made an unforgettable impression on the Spaniards. For she was very beautiful, walking slowly into the great house, looking as a queen should at the people around her. As she came upon the dais, her naked charms were plain to be seen. Over her breasts lay a necklace of golden beads, and at her throat she wore a handsome collar of pearls and stones.

Menéndez took her hand and seated her between Carlos and the sister. Again he referred to his paper, which gave him the words to tell her that she was very beautiful. At this, she looked at her husband and blushed very prettily. Carlos frowned, and ordered her to go.

But Menéndez resorted to the interpreter and persuaded Carlos to let her stay, and sent at once for the gifts he had brought.

First there was a chemise for each of the two women. When these white garments were upon the dark-skinned ladies, green gowns were produced and draped upon them. Then came beads, and gifts of scissors, knives, bells, and last of all, mirrors. Carlos too received a garment, as well as a pair of hatchets and a machete, and little presents were given to the principal men and women in the gathering.

Carlos was unhappy no longer. He ordered the food brought in. It turned out to be varieties of roasted or boiled fish, and oysters prepared as one preferred — raw, boiled, or roasted.

54

To this simple fare the Spaniards added the touch of another civilization: a table was set up for the four people on the dais. It was spread with a cloth and furnished with napkins. A quantity of biscuit was brought and divided among the principal Indians. Bottles of wine and honey were put on the table, and sweetmeats and quince preserves.

As the food was being carried in, the trumpeters sounded a flourish, and the Spanish orchestra began a concert. The dwarf danced with the music; and when he was done, a half dozen of the Spanish gentlemen sang in ensemble.

The Indians were ecstatic; and at seeing them so, Menéndez was doubly merry. He liked good music and had around him the best musicians he could find. At Carlos' request, the musicians continued the performance; but at last the meal was finished, the napkins used, and the table removed.

"Well," said Menéndez, "I must go."

"I have given you my sister," said Carlos affably, "and you may take her away."

There was no way out of it. Menéndez took the hand of his bride and, followed by a contingent of natives, walked with her down the path to the harbor.

The Spanish women took the Princess in hand. After being washed, she was baptized. Saint Anthony's aid in finding the castaways was duly acknowledged by calling the harbor San Antón, and giving the Princess the name of Antonia.

Antonia was placed under the care of Captain de las Alas, who was to sail directly to Havana. There Antonia and her cortège would be instructed in religion, under the guardianship of Juan de Hinestrosa. De las Alas would use the opportunity to pick up cattle and poultry, if they could be obtained, and continue on to St. Augustine.

Menéndez arrived at St. Augustine on March 20, 1566. The first winter had been hard for the little settlement. Food was scarce, the weather cold, and spirits low. Many people had died. A hundred men had mutinied and fled to the Caribbean. Nor was the trouble over, by any means. When Menéndez urged his plan to explore the northern coast and plant another base, another hundred deserted. Since there had also been mutiny and desertions at San Mateo his forces were seriously weakened. Fortunately the Asturian newcomers replaced some of the losses.

He decided to leave one hundred and fifty men at St. Augustine, reinforce San Mateo to the same number, and use the remaining hundred and fifty in the exploration. As before, two *bergantines* would do the inshore work, while a larger vessel supported them from deeper waters. Their interpreter was a French youth named William Rufin, who had lived among the natives of the upper coast.

They left St. Augustine late in March. Spring was beginning to dress the stark branches of the deciduous trees, and new growth highlighted the dark evergreens. On the sea, the wind was no longer full of winter. San Mateo was the first stop, and loyal Villaroel and his handful of men were immensely relieved to have the reinforcements and supplies.

On April 1 the expedition again got under way. Three days later the *bergantines* were in a harbor on the Georgia coast. The mother ship waited at sea.

Menéndez moored the two craft at a landing near a village, which almost immediately emitted a sizeable party of Indians. They came pelting down the trail toward the strange vessels, and their unfriendliness was plain to see. The arquebusiers made ready.

The Indians stopped a little distance away. One stepped forward, naked like the others and carrying bow and arrows. But when he spoke, it was in fluent Spanish.

He turned out to be one of Ribault's interpreters who had survived the shipwreck. From him they learned that Guale was the name of the cacique and his village.

"If your Indians want to eat," said Menéndez, "have them come."

There were forty of them. Somewhat hesitantly they came to the beach. Putting aside their bows, they sat on the sand. The Spaniards fed them biscuit and dried figs, which they ate with a will. After the food, presents were given out. The last semblance of hostility vanished, and before long Menéndez with four halberdiers and thirty arquebusiers, escorted by the forty Indians, started toward the village.

The cacique himself, who was an old man, came forth to greet them. At his side were two of his sons and several advisers. The Spaniards were greeted in peace and quartered in a hut.

From the interpreter, Menéndez learned that Guale was at war with Orista, cacique of the northerly land they wished to explore. Guale had captured two of Orista's kinsmen, and proposed to sacrifice them to the rain gods.

After talking with Guale, Menéndez had a large cross erected in the village, and the Spaniards came together and sang the litanies; and when they kissed the cross, Guale and all his people did the same.

Menéndez explained to the old man that in order to bring peace between Guale and Orista, he wanted to take the two captives back to Orista. Guale spoke with his advisers, and shook his head.

"I cannot consent. Orista does not want our friendship, and will take his kinspeople away from you.

"For eight months," he went on, "no rain has fallen. Our fields are dried up; we are sad, because there is little food. No, it is better to keep the men of Orista and sacrifice them to the rain gods."

"Not so!" cried Menéndez, when the Frenchman had translated. "God denies you water because you are at war, and because you kill your captives."

And he went on to say that he would give hostages from among his own men. "These you can kill," he said, "if I fail to make peace with Orista and do not return you the prisoners."

To this, Guale agreed. So, leaving six people with old Guale, and taking one of his Indians as envoy along with the pair of captives, the Spaniards boarded the *bergantines* the next morning. They had been in the harbor four days instead of the two or three hours that Captain de las Alas had expected; but he was still waiting at anchor. They reached him at noon, and he welcomed them with trumpets and artillery salutes. The concussion of the guns distressed the Indians, who explained they hurt both the head and the heart.

"Sound the trumpets," said they. "That is good. But not the cannon."

"Let it be so," said Menéndez with a laugh. And to his interpreter he exclaimed, "William, talk to these Indians! You understand them, so cheer them up as best you can." And turning to the soldiers around them, he charged them likewise to take good care of their guests.

The next afternoon they arrived at the point of Santa Elena (which is today Hilton Head, South Carolina); and thanks to their Indian passengers, who were good fishermen and knew the waters well, they were guided into the harbor and up a river. After sailing for a league they anchored the ship and continued in the *bergantines,* carrying fifty men in each.

For quite a distance they ascended the river, until at last they sighted the village of Orista. It was an unhappy vista of grey ashes and charred posts. Guale raiders had burned it, the Spaniards learned later. Here and there a new hut was going up, but there were not many people about.

A few came out, all excited and ready to loose their arrows at the first target.

"They believe you are some of the wicked ones who captured us," the two Orista captives explained to Menéndez. "We shall go tell them you are good people, and explain why you came."

Menéndez set them ashore, and soon he landed all his men, except for a guard of ten men in each *bergantín*. And then the village Indians came, leaving their weapons behind and greeting Menéndez with the utmost humility and respect.

The next day they went to a nearby village to meet Orista. The cacique arrived with two of his head men, and all were plainly glad to see William, who had married one of Orista's daughters during his previous sojourn in this land.

William told them to call the principal Indians together so Menéndez could speak, and the conclave was soon ready. Conspicuously present were the three — the pair of Orista's men and the envoy from Guale — brought by Menéndez.

"Now, William," instructed Menéndez, "tell them everything that happened in Guale about making peace."

This took a while, and when the youth was finished, Orista sent him away so that he might not hear the debate of the council. It was half an hour before they called him back for more talk. At last William turned again to Menéndez and said:

"He is glad to make peace. He will be even more pleased to become a true Christian." With a grin William explained: "He says the men of Guale want to do this, and they are no better than the people of Orista."

Menéndez was inspired to launch into explanation of the Faith, and his homily was well received.

"I cannot live here," he concluded, "but I wish I could stay and teach you to become Christians, so that you could go to heaven."

"Then leave someone to teach us," said they; and so earnest was the plea that Menéndez agreed to do so.

After the sermon it was time for the feast. The women came, bearing maize, boiled and roasted fish, oysters, and acorns; and not to be outdone, Menéndez put biscuit and honey and wine on the board, to be divided among the Indians. They were ecstatic over the biscuit dipped in honey-water.

It was a happy, noisy meal, with much talk and shouts of laughter. Then came the singing and dancing. The principal Indians took places beside Menéndez to watch. Not until midnight did the party end.

The place Orista recommended for the colony was on a low island beside the channel, about a league inside the harbor, and visible from the sea. Broad marshes isolated it from the mainland. The land was low, except for an elevation where they could build a fort, and densely forested.

To the Spaniards it seemed a good location. The captains planned and marked out the fort. Captain Antonio Gómez, a good artilleryman, was in charge of the construction. Within fifteen days it was defensible — a palisaded earthwork mounting six cannon. They named it San Felipe (Saint Philip), and the harbor Santa Elena. A hundred and ten men were assigned as garrison under Captain de las Alas. One of the *bergantines* sailed back to San Mateo and St. Augustine with the news of what had taken place. The ship was dispatched with twenty men to Santo Domingo for a cargo of supplies.

With the remaining *bergantín*, Menéndez began the return to Guale. Aboard her were his twenty remaining soldiers, William the interpreter, and a pair of Orista's Indians who would complete the peace talks with Guale.

On May 8 they anchored again at Guale's village. Menéndez disembarked with the envoys from Orista and met Guale in council. The envoys talked peace so that all were pleased. Yet it was plain that old Cacique Guale was preoccupied by another matter. Presently he began to talk.

"I have made peace with Orista, as you said, that God might not be angry." And now the aged one looked at Menéndez, imploring help: "Do you therefore beseech God to give water for my fields and gardens. For nine months it has not rained."

Menéndez could find only an evasive answer. "God commanded you to do many things you have not done," he said. "For this reason He will not give you rain, though I besought him to do so."

The old man turned away sadly and went slowly to his house. There two Spanish lads, whom Menéndez had left in the village to teach the Doctrine to the Indians, found him. Guale's interpreter was with them.

"Do not be sad," they told him. "We will pray for rain."

Guale was overjoyed. In an excess of appreciation, he loaded the youngsters with deerskins and maize and fish. But the word soon got to Menéndez, who was in no mood to let these mischievous boys trifle with the cacique. The precious pair were forced to give up their loot, and they were stripped of their shirts for a whipping, near the big cross in the midst of the village.

It was about two in the afternoon, and the entire population gathered to see what was going on. The cacique quickly understood the meaning of the boys' naked backs and taut faces, and he went to Menéndez.

"You deceive me," he said accusingly. "You would not ask the Cacique of Heaven for rain, and now you will whip the boys because they did so."

Menéndez said nothing.

"Do not whip them," Guale said, hope gone from his voice. "I no longer want them to pray. I am content to wait for rain when God wills it."

Menéndez was indignant at the interpretation the old Indian put on the matter.

"These rogues have tricked you," he expostulated.

Nevertheless, he let them go. They would give no further trouble.

To Cacique Guale he said impatiently: "If you want to be a true Christian, God will give rain to you sooner than to me or these boys with their lies."

Guale was perplexed. "But I have been a true Christian since the very first day," he said.

He looked at the cross. His shuffling steps raised the dust as he went directly to this symbol of the Faith. He knelt on the parched earth and kissed the rough wood. Then he stood erect, and looked at Menéndez.

"Behold," he said, "how I am a true Christian."

The people slowly dispersed. None thought to look at the sky until, about half an hour later, the wind came and thunder sounded and lightning played in towering black clouds that obscured the sun.

The rain came down hard, and with it a great thunderbolt that splintered a tall tree on the edge of the village. Men and women, rejoicing in the downpour, ran to snatch away the splinters and take them to their huts as visible evidence of the omnipotence of the Cacique of Heaven.

The news of the miraculous rain — for the downpour had occurred only in Guale's region — preceded the Spaniards like a bow wave on their way south. And since they were sailing the inland passage behind the coastal islands, they were often intercepted by Indians who paddled their canoes out to welcome them. Menéndez developed a routine of landing, giving out presents, and erecting a small cross in each village.

SYMBOL OF THE FAITH

Into the Back Country

THE IDYLLIC springtime voyage down the waterway, past friendly aboriginal villages came abruptly to an end on May 15, 1566, as the *bergantín* anchored in the dark waters of the St. Johns at San Mateo. The first word from the fort was that all of Saturiba's Indians were on the war path. The fort at St. Augustine had been burned. It was worth your life to go into the woods.

Fighting the Indians in the wilderness was a nerve-wracking experience for soldiers schooled in the formality of European tactics. The strain lay heavily upon Villaroel, the commander. Indians who came to the fort expected to barter for food, clothes and other articles. When there was nothing for them, they turned ugly. Here and at St. Augustine, the casualty list had already mounted to a hundred men.

Menéndez asked what was being done to punish the Indians.

"You can't fight them," wearily said Villaroel. "When you aim at one with the arquebus, he just backs off and watches you. The prime flashes — he ducks and crawls through the grass (this country is nothing but high grass and woods), and your target is gone. After the shot hits harmlessly where he *was*, he comes up in a different place. Really, the way they do it is worth seeing.

"And once you've fired, he'll have four or five arrows off before you can reload. They shoot fast, and they shoot hard. The arrows penetrate even our mail shirts."

"What can be done?" asked Menéndez.

"The only way to beat them," his officer answered, "is to go to their villages. You cut down their plantings, burn their huts, take the canoes, and destroy the fishways. These are the only properties they have. Either they keep their word with us, or they must leave the land."

Menéndez took only the time needed to load his vessel with supplies San Mateo could spare for St. Augustine before he was on the way. On May 18 the *bergantín* joined the two other craft that were at anchor in front of the village of St. Augustine.

The blackened scar of the burnt fort was at once apparent. The Spaniards hastened ashore to embrace their welcomers and join in the exchange of tears and laughter.

The population was gathered at the shore, and Menéndez talked to them a few minutes, telling of the fine beginnings at Guale and Santa Elena. Then he had the men unload the food and gunpowder brought from San Mateo.

He wasted very little time inspecting the ruins of the fortification. His brother Bartolomé told him the Indians had twice come upon them by night. Out of the darkness hissed the arrows; two of the sentinels were killed.

"On the second night they shot fire arrows," he said. "Flames started at once in the thatch roof. The wind spread them. Control was impossible.

"We lost everything — powder, munitions, cloth, flags and standards — yours as well as those won from the French. Nothing escaped."

Valdés said, "We were in real trouble, being without food. A man goes out for palm cabbage or oysters, he comes back with a skin full of arrows. A few Indians are always ready to set up an ambush," he concluded irritably.

Menéndez brought Valdés and the captains together. Choosing a better site for the fort should have been done long ago, anyhow; and wise with the lesson taught by the fire arrows of the Timucua, they resolved to build the new fort on Anastasia Island, near the channel and as far as possible from the Indians.

The construction officer divided them into four gangs, and the work into four parts. Casts of the dice determined which part fell to each gang. They worked from three in the morning until nine, and again in the afternoon from two until six, avoiding the hot, humid hours before the seabreeze came, and the overhead noontime sun. Within ten days the artillery was moved across the bay from the old site to the new, and was in position. The fort was defensible, though not yet finished.

None of the vessels sent for provisions had returned; and as the stock of food dwindled, the colonists were again on the verge of desperation. So it was agreed that Menéndez would take the *bergantin* on a fast run to Havana. They left the harbor just in time to aid an incoming supply vessel that missed the channel and almost ran aground. Otherwise the voyage was without incident except for gale winds and high seas in the Strait.

Havana harbor was a proud sight. The treasure fleet was in, and the spars of more than thirty vessels formed a tracery against the tropic sky. However, Menéndez again had little success in raising funds to provision the King's soldiers (who had been fed out of his own pocket for the past eight months), nor in rounding up Florida deserters who had found their way to Cuba.

Discouraged, he talked to his good friend Hinestrosa, who promised to find help. Then he went to the house of Alonso de Rojas, who was the Havana guardian of Antonia, the Indian princess. With him he took a number of friends, and some musicians to liven up the party.

Antonia seemed glad to see him, but despite the gay talk and the animation of her visitors, she soon lapsed into depression. Menéndez turned to the interpreter, who was one of the Spanish women rescued from Carlos.

"Pray have Antonia tell me why she is sad," he said.

It took many urgings, but at last Antonia said in a low voice: "Tell him I want to die. He did not send for me to come to his house, to eat and sleep with him."

Menéndez, disconcerted by this frankness, searched for an excuse.

"When we wear this cross," he said, pointing to the symbol on his doublet (for he was a knight of the Order of Santiago), "and are returning from battle, we may not sleep with our wives for eight days."

He looked into her face, and added gently, "Tell her I wish the eight days were gone, for I love her very much."

Antonia was between tears and laughter. "Ah," she said, "could I believe you, I would be happy."

"Then be happy," he said. "I speak the truth."

Antonia laughed and began to count on her fingers.

"Two days are gone already; six more and I will come to your house!"

"See that you do," Menéndez smiled, and he arose, and Antonia came and embraced him, and took his hands.

"Play the music," she cried, and the musicians struck up a tune. Her change in mood cheered everyone.

After an hour, Menéndez asked Antonia if she had any desire to go back to Florida. She was delighted and begged to go, and he promised they would start the next day. And thus he took leave of her and went to his inn.

It had been a long day, and he was tired. By midnight he was in bed, fast asleep. A single candle burned quietly, deepening the shadows in the room.

At the house of Rojas, Antonia aroused herself. She took the maidservant, one of her own people, and went stealthily to the Spanish woman who was her friend and interpreter.

"Come," she whispered. "My husband told me to come to his house. You must go with me."

Her friend quickly dressed for the street, and the three women went out silently into the night. The inn they sought was close by, and the door opened under their insistent knocking. The doorkeeper stared a moment until he recognized the Spanish woman.

"Don Pedro ordered me to come here with Doña Antonia," she told him briskly. And he, with no misgivings, bade them come in, and conducted them to the bedroom.

Antonia softly opened the door, and entered with her two companions. The man in bed breathed steadily in sleep. Seeing the candle, Antonia took it up and shone the light upon the bed. For a long moment she looked at Menéndez. Around the bed and even under it she searched. No, the man had no bed mate.

Menéndez opened his eyes to see Antonia beside the bed with the candle. At the same instant he perceived the others standing at the closed door.

"What is this, sister?" he asked Antonia's friend.

The woman looked indignantly at Antonia, who had calmly seated herself at the head of the bed, still holding the candle.

"Excellency," she faltered, "she told me you ordered her brought to you at this hour. I — I believed her."

Menéndez' expression changed from puzzlement to comprehension, and he roared with laughter. Perhaps the youth in the vestibule smiled to himself at the sound.

When he could speak, Menéndez said, "Tell Doña Antonia that I would surely be glad if the eight days were gone."

"Only let me lie in a corner of the bed," begged Antonia, "so my brother may know we have slept together." Her face betrayed her feelings, as she added: "Otherwise my brother will think you scorn me, and will refuse to be a true friend, or to become a Christian."

Menéndez called for his servant and put him to rummaging in a chest. Each of the three women was presented with a chemise and mirrors and beads, and ushered out of the bedroom.

As they returned to the house of Rojas, Antonia's friend wondered what they would have done if Menéndez had not awakened.

"Why," said Antonia complacently, "I would have put out the candle and lay down beside him."

They left Havana as planned. It took three days to reach the harbor of San Antón. They dropped anchor at the port entrance, because Menéndez did not dare go up to Carlos' town with no more than the thirty soldiers and sailors he had.

Antonia sent for Carlos. Within a couple of hours he arrived with an escort of a dozen canoes, including a pair tied together as a royal barge, the decks shaded by mats draped over a tunnel of hoops. With a sigh of relief, Menéndez entrusted Antonia to her brother, and went back to Havana.

In that city, Hinestrosa's efforts had not been very successful, aside from collecting a little money to buy meat and cassava. So Menéndez, like many others have done before and since, took his problem to the moneylenders; and for a fine gold-embroidered suit and various other personal articles, he obtained five hundred ducats. The money brought a few more provisions.

Nothing more could be done, except get these supplies to Florida as soon as possible. Three vessels would make the trip: a *fragata, bergantín* and *patache*. They sailed July 1, going out from Havana with the vessels of the treasure fleet, which was beginning the long voyage to Spain.

But as the convoy swept into the Bahama Channel and slowly worked itself into the great crescent sailing formation, the three little Florida vessels pushed on ahead. For Menéndez was impatient with the pace of the convoy, and anxious to see his people. The depression that had been with him ashore lifted, as always, when a deck was beneath his feet.

He kept the vessel well out in the current of the Gulf Stream and made good time. On July 8 they headed inshore. The landfall was the mouth of the St. Johns.

At anchor off the bar was a ship. Her crew said she was one of seventeen come from Spain with fifteen hundred soldiers. In the best of spirits, Menéndez took his vessel over the bar and upriver to San Mateo. In a field camp outside the fort were about two hundred and fifty men — new arrivals, it appeared from their dress. Within the fort were the tattered Florida veterans.

The main body of the expedition was at St. Augustine, and Menéndez chafed to get there. Commander of the reinforcements was Sancho de Arciniega, an old friend, and he looked forward to seeing him again. And there would be mail from Spain.

It was not yet dark when they reached St. Augustine. But since Arciniega was still aboard ship, they did not see each other until the next morning. The greeting was affectionate, as befitted a reunion between old friends, and Arciniega was in jovial mood as he gave over the royal dispatches, the armada, and the men.

Fourteen women had come with the expedition, and when the council ended, Menéndez went to meet these brave females. They were all gathered at one house for the occasion and they were naïvely pleased with his words of welcome. He also talked with the five priests who had come, and assigned Father López as their vicar.

But the good news was tempered with bad. Valdés, the young fieldmaster, said the Indians had taken Ochoa in ambush, woodsman though he was. Others had died at his side.

"They were good men," said Menéndez, "and I loved them. At Fort Caroline they were among the first to attack. Through all the hardship and danger they have been willing and loyal."

"We had no food," said Valdés miserably. "We had to gather oysters and palm cabbage. Always many of us foraged together, for those who went alone never came back."

Gently Menéndez said, "I am very sorry. But in our work, death and hardship and danger cannot be avoided. May God reward these brave soldiers."

The defense they had built a few weeks earlier was already undermined by the sea. Menéndez and certain of the captains chose a safer site farther inland, and marked out the trace for the new fort. As before, they divided the men and the work into sections, then let casts of the dice decide the assignments.

The bells rang at dawn on the morrow, and the drums beat the muster. It was good to see the men come hurrying to work. The job went well.

Of the fifteen hundred new soldiers half would be stationed in Florida at St. Augustine, San Mateo and Santa Elena. Menéndez would take the remaining seven hundred fifty men and eight vessels to fortify the islands of Puerto Rico, Hispaniola and Cuba, and drive out the corsairs. Arciniega would shepherd the rest of the armada back to Spain.

Before leaving Florida again, however, Menéndez wanted to inspect the posts at San Mateo and Santa Elena. And upon reaching the St. Johns, he decided to follow its course to see if it was the hoped-for waterway to the land of Carlos, far to the southwest. It was high time, too, that he met the caciques in this river country, and laid the groundwork for friendship.

So upriver they went, a hundred men in three *bergantines*, guided by an Indian interpreter. Against the current, progress was slow; but by midnight of the second day they were twenty leagues from San Mateo, and not far from the town of the Cacique Otina. At one in the morning they landed. The guide led them through level lands toward the settlement.

Envoys who went ahead reached the village after daybreak. Otina was at home. Menéndez and twenty others would be welcome, he said. And since Otina had heard of the rain miracle in Guale, he suggested that Menéndez might also pray for rain here. The cornfields had been dry for six months.

By the time the messengers made their way back, the main force was a scant quarter league from the town. Menéndez was quite pleased with Otina's attitude, and readily agreed to halt most of his men on the trail.

On he went with twenty, laughing at Otina's message about rain. But the closer they came to the town, the darker grew the sky; and when they marched into the town, the downpour started. Yet the place was strangely quiet and empty, except for a few warriors who were nervously watching from a distance.

The guide led them to Otina's house, but Otina was gone.

"Go find him," directed Menéndez. "Say that I have come with twenty men and the rain."

One of Otina's scouts ran with the message, and soon returned.

"The Cacique Otina is hidden in the forest and will not come," he said. "Otina fears you who have such power with God. He is your friend, and bids you depart."

Menéndez had to be content with charging Otina by messenger to send word of the expedition to the river villages they must pass. Back to the boats they went, and continued upstream about fifty leagues to the territory of the Cacique Macoya, who was known to be a friend to their enemy Saturiba.

Macoya sent word that his warriors were angry because the Spaniards had come to their land without permission, so they must turn back. Though the day was growing late, Menéndez was determined to push on. He ordered the sweeps out, and the men rowed for a league, the river becoming more and more narrow. Along the shore they could see armed warriors who seemed to be working themselves into a fine state of excitement. Ahead, the river banks came together in a narrow pass, and this pass had been obstructed by a row of stakes. The current, sluggish up to now, grew swift.

They reached the line of stakes and broke through. The men strained at the sweeps and the craft inched onward against the hurrying water. For now the river was deep and narrow, so narrow that two pikes would span it. The Spaniards looked apprehensively at the dense summer growth along the banks. The oarsmen would be perfect targets for Indian bowmen.

Two warriors showed themselves on the bank. They brought an ultimatum.

"Cacique Macoya tells you to go no farther. You must turn back. If not, we begin war with you."

It was a moment of extreme peril. For if they pushed on, the deadly arrow flights were certain. If they retreated, the Indians might interpret the withdrawal as a sign of cowardice, and attack anyway.

Assuming a carelessness he did not feel, Menéndez spoke to the interpreter.

"Tell them they can start war whenever they wish. While I did not come here to harm them, I must go up this river. Yet say also that now it is night, and I will stay here until morning."

Perhaps the boldness of the reply saved them. The night descended, and there was no attack.

It began to rain, and it rained hard. There was little shelter and the arquebusiers cursed as the wetness got to the match-cords and powder. The guns were useless.

So the decision was made for him. Menéndez ordered the *bergantines* to retire quietly. They found the break in the line of stakes and slipped through it.

Some days later they came again to the landing in Otina's territory. Once more a meeting with Otina was arranged, and this time the cacique came with three hundred warriors. Cautiously they stopped a quarter league from the Spanish vessels. Menéndez took twenty of his best arquebusiers and marched them smartly (and noisily) to the rendezvous.

The little company halted within range of the warriors, who surrounded their leader in such fashion that the Spaniards could not see him. Menéndez chose two soldiers and the interpreter, and walked toward the dusky phalanx.

The ranks parted to reveal a central space, in the middle of which, on the ground, sat a young man about twenty-five years of age. Like his warriors, he was naked except for the breechclout.

He greeted Menéndez gravely and with respect, and the others one by one followed his example. Menéndez was quite prepared for the occasion. He dressed Otina in breeches and doublet of green silk, and put a hat on his head. The outfit was quite becoming; the Spaniards said that Otina really had the face and figure of a gentleman.

On the thirteenth day, the expedition was back at San Mateo. Menéndez stayed only long enough to make final arrangements for sending a few men to begin a mission and settlement in the Chesapeake Bay country. (However, all later turned up in Sevilla, saying that a storm had prevented their planting the colony.)

From San Mateo, Menéndez went to Santa Elena. In all, he was there eight days, planning assignments and new explorations. Captain Juan Pardo would take a hundred and fifty men into the woodlands to the west. At a suitable location he would build a fort, and begin to teach the natives. Pardo's report on the country might be of vital importance in resettling the Spanish farmers, who found the sandy soil of the coast little to their liking.

Finally, Menéndez called all the men together, and talked about the work to be done. And having charged them to be steadfast in the King's service, he left Santa Elena at the end of August in 1566.

The voyage southward to Guale, where Menéndez had won his reputation as a rainmaker, took two days. They stayed a week or so, renewing friendships with the caciques. Another two-day voyage brought the Spaniards back to San Mateo; and from there they went on to St. Augustine.

Poor Valdés was in trouble again. It was the usual rebellion against the hardships of frontier duty, with no prospects of winning wealth in this far province of Spain's America. Three of the mutineers had been hanged; others were imprisoned. Pedro de Rodabán, one of Arciniega's captains, was among them.

70

"Rodabán is their leader," said Valdés bitterly. "He is the one who caused the mutiny. He gave the order that started it."

Menéndez' investigation showed cause for the charge, true enough. But he counseled with his young commander, pointing out that soldiers from Spain needed time to adjust to the rigors of Florida service.

"Valdés, we do not know these new captains and their men very well," he said. "Since so many of them refused to obey orders, we are faced with doing what *can* be done, rather than what *should* be done. You have heard me say before that sometimes it is necessary to overlook what cannot be helped. So for the sake of peace, it is proper for me to reprimand Rodabán, and then free him. Yet the charge against him shall stand."

Valdés said, perhaps reluctantly, "That is fair enough."

With the release of the prisoners, once again matters were set straight for a while.

For the Cacique of Heaven

AND NOW it was high time to move against the corsairs in the Antilles, as Philip had charged Menéndez to do along with the Florida project. The expedition was outfitted, the captains chosen. All told, there were eight vessels. On October 20, 1566, the corsair hunters slipped out of St. Augustine harbor and turned their prows toward the Caribbean.

No place was safe from the corsairs. The tropic isles were ideal for hiding and harboring sea robbers.

And for the ones who were strong enough to bluster ashore and sack or seize poorly defended towns for ransom, there was also a great deal of reward. Still others hit upon surer ways to make profit. The needs of the Spanish towns and the plantations were many, and Spanish ships could not supply them all. Enterprising Englishmen like John Hawkins — and French and Portuguese captains too — furnished goods ranging from African slaves to Flemish lace, and thought of themselves as honest traders who turned to corsairing only when the occasion demanded.

The foreign vessels in turn were fair game for Spanish captains not averse to risking a battle for the profit a prize might bring. There was, from the Spanish viewpoint, no question of legality. Spanish America was closed to foreigners by edict; therefore any foreign craft in Caribbean waters must be either smuggler or corsair.

At times, a prize might bring a fortune to its captors. Vessels emptied of slaves or merchandise were apt to be heavy with gold received in exchange. But by the time trading was done, summer was gone. Rather than risk the tempestuous Atlantic, the astute businessmen wintered in the tropics. They had favorite places of rendezvous: northern Hispaniola; Mona Island, west of Puerto Rico; and San Germán, on Puerto Rico's western coast.

It was to these places that Menéndez directed his attention. With almost a thousand men and the little armada, he could handle any nest of corsairs he was liable to find. Afterward, the soldiers could be stationed where they were needed from Cuba to Puerto Rico, and the armada disbanded.

On November 5 Menéndez reached Mona Island with three of his fleet. Valdés with the rest went on to San Germán. The corsairs were gone from both places, but at San Germán there was disturbing news.

Late in September, it was said, an armada of twenty-seven armed ships, bearing six thousand soldiers, had left France. They had taken Madeira. Surely they were bound next for America! Valdés sent the intelligence to Menéndez at once.

Characteristically, Menéndez moved quickly. He sent his ships to Valdés at San Germán, with orders to careen and grease them and condition the entire armada for action. Then he journeyed westward to confer with the district officials at Santo Domingo, which was a thing Philip had instructed him to do.

After proper discussion, the council, as one would expect, made a conservative decision. It was duly expressed by the president:

"Our advice is to fortify this city, and the cities of San Juan in Puerto Rico and Havana in Cuba, as well as neighboring ports, which is what our King ordered you to do. Then you should return with all speed to Florida."

The recommendation disappointed Menéndez. He much preferred to seek out and destroy the cause of the threat.

Concealing his disappointment as best he could, he asked the officials to meet with him for planning and inspection. That afternoon and the next day he worked them hard, deciding upon the best methods of strengthening the fort and fortifying the city; examining the terrain to anticipate enemy landings, and stationing sentries; inspecting the artillery, and providing for repairs and new emplacements.

In getting this work planned and under way, Menéndez spent less than a week at Santo Domingo, after which he joined Valdés at San Germán. Valdés had done a good job. The armada was ready for action. Perhaps some were disappointed on learning they would not sail against the French, but Menéndez gave them no time to think about it.

Weapons and munitions were dispatched to Santo Domingo. To San Juan, Menéndez sent a hundred arquebusiers by sea, with powder and four cannon. He himself also went to San Juan, but he went the shortest, fastest route, which was overland.

73

The townspeople welcomed him with open arms — or at least those who were left did so; most of them had fled to the woods with their children and goods at the news that the French armada was coming. Nor had the Governor been able to get them back. But when word of the reinforcements went out, the citizens flocked back to the city, and had rejoicings, and prayers for victory, and made brave pronouncements that they would die rather than surrender to the enemy.

Menéndez met with the Governor and other officials, including the commander of the fort (who was Juan Ponce de León, grandson of the Juan Ponce noted as the discoverer and first governor of Florida). He inspected the fort on the harbor. Then he went to El Morro, the high headland above the narrow entrance to the bay. It was defended by a tower, and he made important suggestions for improvement. He visited other sites where an enemy might disembark, and consulted with the officials in working out practical plans for fortification and defense.

On the fourth day, Menéndez traveled back to San Germán, and soon afterward worked his way methodically westward, touching at all the ports likely to be molested by the French, until by January 1567 he was back at Havana. In hardly more than two months (for they had left St. Augustine late in October) the expedition had traveled some two thousand miles, strengthening the defenses in a dozen towns from San Juan to Havana. It was too bad, in a way, that the French armada never came.

Antonia was in Havana. Captain Reinoso had brought her. As instructed, he had gone to Charlotte Harbor with the messages and presents Menéndez had sent. Then, leaving his thirty soldiers quartered in a house built for them by the Indians, he took Antonia and some of the principal Indians to Havana.

Again had Don Alonso de Rojas and his wife warmly welcomed Antonia into their home. Reinoso returned at once to Charlotte Harbor, stopping only to load livestock and supplies. Menéndez reached Havana soon afterward, but the chronicler gives us no word of his meetings with Antonia. However, on March 1, 1567, they sailed for Charlotte Harbor.

This time the fleet consisted of six *pataches* and *bergantines* from Havana. They carried a hundred and fifty soldiers. It was a good passage; they were at Charlotte Harbor in two days, and landed amidst a jubilant welcome. Work began at once on a chapel for Father Juan Rogel, one of the Jesuit missionaries, and near it a house for Antonia, as Menéndez had promised her. They were unpretentious structures in the Indian style, and quickly finished. On the next day, the good Father offered Mass and preached to the soldiers.

"They have sore need of a sermon," sighed Captain Reinoso.

Menéndez looked at him with mild surprise.

"They need to be taught," Reinoso went on. "We hope you will leave Father Rogel with us for a good example of how a Christian should live. Otherwise we shall soon be savages ourselves."

"Why?" asked Menéndez.

Reinoso, a little sheeepishly, said, "The reason is—well, the Indian women love us passionately. It has reached the point where — if you had not come — Carlos and his men were going to kill us. Even if Doña Antonia and her people had to die too, Carlos was ready to kill us all. We are not dead because the women had warned us, and we are very careful."

"What have you learned about the waterway we look for?" asked Menéndez, who was determined this time to find the supposed connection with the St. Johns River.

"You will find a river fifty leagues to the north," said Reinoso. "It is in a land they call Tocobaga."

The captain had much more to say about the habits and customs of the Indians, and Menéndez was both pleased and troubled to learn that while most of them seemed devout enough before the cross of the Faith, Carlos himself had become scornful and troublesome.

However, the cacique now seemed very glad to see Menéndez again. Twice they dined together, the two leaders and the principal men and women; and the subject of an expedition to Tocobaga received considerable attention.

"Tocobaga is an enemy," said Carlos. "He has made war on me. Now you can go with me and my men to make war on him."

Menéndez said, "My master, the King of Spain, did not send me here to make war on the caciques. Rather, if the caciques are quarreling I must try to make them friends, and ask them if they want to become Christians. If so, I will teach them the doctrine which shows the manner of going at last to the Cacique of Heaven, who is also Master of all the earth.

"Therefore," he concluded, "I want to be a friend to Tocobaga. I will speak to him of peace."

Carlos was obviously disappointed. Nevertheless, he offered to accompany the Spaniards to Tocobaga.

On March 5 all six vessels sailed northward for Tampa Bay, which they reached on the moonless night of the second day. Carlos and twenty of his head men were aboard, including a guide who was so skillful that he brought them into the harbor and up the bay to anchor quietly in front of Tocobaga's town before daybreak.

Amazingly, the anchorage was made without waking the town. When Carlos realized this, he came at once to Menéndez.

"Put me and my men on the land," he whispered fiercely. "We will burn the cacique's house, and swim back here."

Menéndez shook his head. "I will not let you do it," he said sternly. "You came with me only to talk of peace and friendship."

The young cacique was not used to having his wishes thwarted, and a flood of anger swept over him. But the sound of his rage only drew the soldiers who would enforce Menéndez' decision. Like a wilful child, he wept.

When he would listen again, Menéndez reminded him that his sister and several others were held captive by Tocobaga.

"I will try to make an honorable peace between you and Tocobaga," he said earnestly, "so that he will give your people back."

"That will be good," said Carlos, brightening. "I am satisfied."

It was almost light, and the town would soon be astir. The women would come sleepily out of the huts, their eyes widening as they saw foreign ships right in front of their homes. Menéndez had no wish to terrorize these people. He called a Spaniard who had been a slave of the Indians and knew the language of Tocobaga, and sent him ashore in an eight-oared tender.

The man left the boat and walked quietly to the house of the Cacique Tocobaga. He halted in front of the doorway, sucked in his breath, and in a loud voice began his proclamation.

"Fear not, O people of Tocobaga, have no fear!"

His bellowing did nothing to reassure the sleep-befuddled inhabitants. Heads popped out of doorways before the pronouncement was through. In the misty dawn light the Spanish vessels, where last night there were none, were a fearsome sight. In less time than it takes to tell, the town was empty, the people fled to the shelter of the forest.

Yet, one house had not emptied. It was the house of Tocobaga. With his favorite wife and a few companions, he stayed quietly inside despite the frenzied flight of his people. At eight o'clock Menéndez landed and made his way to the cacique's house. Tocobaga, with his wife and six head men, greeted Menéndez warmly. They talked at some length, and at last Menéndez said:

"I am a friend to Carlos, and some of our Christians now live in his land. Carlos is aboard my vessel now. I brought him to talk with you of peace and friendship. For your part, you should release the twelve of his people that you hold captive.

"And if you wish," he continued, "I will leave some of my men with you, as I did with Carlos, so they can defend you from your enemies, and teach you the Faith."

The suggestion that foreigners come among them to live and to teach new ways was too important a matter for hasty decision.

"My head men and the caciques who are my friends and subjects are far away," Tocobaga replied. "I cannot answer until I summon them here."

So three days passed, and each day more Indians came out of the forest until there must have been fifteen hundred of them, and all warriors, judging by their physiques and the quantity of weapons. This was, in truth, more than Menéndez had bargained for. Outnumbered better than ten to one, his men were getting nervous. Nor did he wish to put his own head into the alligator's mouth. He spoke to Tocobaga.

"If we are to have a peace talk, you had better send all your people away, except the head men."

Tocobaga's probable purpose — a show of strength — had already been achieved. The warriors slipped away. Left for the council were some twenty-nine caciques, each with three or four advisers. On the fourth day they came together. Taking Carlos along, Menéndez went into the assemblage and was duly escorted to a seat where all could see him. Tocobaga spoke directly to him:

"I have told this council of all you said to me. If you have spoken truth, all here will be glad to take you for elder brother, become Christians, make peace with Carlos, and give his people back to him."

Menéndez would have expressed his pleasure, but Tocobaga continued after a glance at Carlos.

"If Carlos again makes war upon me, your soldiers must help me. But should I be the one to break the peace, you shall help Carlos.

"And as you did with Carlos, you shall leave me a captain with thirty men who will teach me and my caciques how to be Christians."

Now Menéndez spoke, agreeing wholeheartedly to these terms. And the peace was made with Carlos, after which his people were returned to him. The council ended in an amiable spirit of brotherhood.

The only disappointment in the outcome of the talks was the plan to explore the waterway to the St. Johns. Tocobaga informed him the trip was impossible without more men. The Indians on the way were hostile and numerous.

On the voyage back to Charlotte Harbor, Carlos showed increasing resentment at the peace, despite the recovery of his sister and the other captives. The unhappy situation came to a head when a sailor chanced to walk by and drop a rope's end on Carlos' head. With a roar of anger the Indian leaped at the unfortunate seaman and struck him a great blow in the face. The man staggered back. Like a bear Carlos was after him. He grappled with him and tried to heave him overboard.

Menéndez, like the others who saw the flare-up, was stunned for an instant. Then he ran to the struggling pair, seized Carlos and wrested him away. By then they were surrounded and Carlos gave up the fight. But his rage was hot as ever, and his eyes held only malice for the Spaniards around him.

The simplest way to cut short Carlos' anger would be to hang him, Menéndez thought grimly. But having agreed to bring him along, he felt duty bound to return him safely. And so it was done. They reached Charlotte Harbor about the middle of March, and Carlos was conveyed to his town as quickly as possible.

With Carlos on the verge of open hostility, Menéndez strengthened Captain Reinoso's little settlement with some additional fortification, a few culverins, and enough soldiers to increase the garrison to fifty. Father Rogel, of course, was staying to teach the Indians.

Antonia had already spoken with her brother, and Menéndez could tell she was angry. No longer demure, she faced him accusingly.

"You made peace with Tocobaga!"

Menéndez admitted it was true.

"You should have killed him!" she cried. "Burned and killed Tocobaga and all his people! Why did you not at least burn the town — and the house of his idols?"

Was this fierce woman the quiet princess who had captivated Havana with her modesty? Menéndez pacified her as best he could, but with indifferent success.

"You have two hearts," she told him at last, resorting to tears. "One is for yourself and the other for Tocobaga. For me and my brother, you have none!"

Menéndez retired without having won the victory, but as always he felt better when he got aboard ship. The last-minute chores before setting sail took a man's mind off his worries.

They were ready to go when a lookout saw a *patache* come into the bay. She brought word from Havana, and it was not good news. Rodabán, the captain he had saved from the death sentence at St. Augustine, was causing trouble at Havana. He was in a conspiracy with Governor Osorio to usurp command of the troops Menéndez had assigned to the Havana defenses.

Menéndez went right back to Havana. Rodabán took to the woods with his supporters, and it was a month before he was finally trapped and brought to judgment.

Exasperated by this second instance of disloyalty, Menéndez sentenced the headstrong captain to decapitation. And Rodabán would have lost his head forthwith, except that advisers persuaded Menéndez to grant an appeal and send him to Spain for trial. This action would avoid any taint of prejudice, they said.

About Osorio, there was nothing to be done, at least not until Menéndez could talk to King Philip. Inasmuch as he had written Philip months ago, saying he would soon be back in Spain, it was high time to get started.

He sailed for Florida, taking a cargo of maize brought from Campeche. The first call was at Tequesta, in southeast Florida. Several Indians from this area who had been with him at Havana and Charlotte Harbor gave a good report to the cacique, and a treaty along the usual pattern was readily agreed upon. Menéndez was now the "elder brother" of most of the important caciques of Florida — except Saturiba.

It was also arranged for Tequesta's brother and two other head men to go with Menéndez to Spain. A complement of thirty men was assigned to the Tequesta station, along with carpenters to build a blockhouse. The work was well under way when Menéndez left.

SATURIBA

This portrait is probably a 17th century copy of a lost original by
Le Moyne. (Courtesy of the National Park Service.)

The weather was fine, and he went directly to San Mateo. It was at the last of April in 1567. Captain Villaroel and his men were healthy, despite continued harassment by the Indians. Saturiba's warriors had killed all their cattle, and seemed on the point of mustering enough braves to slaughter the Spaniards as well.

Although it was now almost two years since the founding of St. Augustine, Menéndez had not yet come face to face with this cacique who controlled the Indians of the lower St. Johns, where the two most important colonies — St. Augustine and San Mateo — had been planted. But at last a good opportunity to bring off a peace conference was at hand. Villaroel had managed to capture sixteen of Saturiba's people, including his son, the Cacique Emoloa. A messenger told Saturiba that Menéndez would be at the river mouth the next morning, enroute to St. Augustine. Let Saturiba meet him at the shore. In due time, word came back. Saturiba would come. Menéndez must bring the prisoners.

In the morning when they reached the mouth of the river, they saw the Indians waiting, but quite far inland. The captives were landed, after proper precautions had been made to prevent their escape or rescue. They were chained, and a *bergantín* was moored close inshore, with twenty arquebusiers at the ready and two half-culverins loaded with small shot.

Saturiba sent a pair of head men, who talked for two hours with Emoloa and his companions. In fact, they talked too much. One of the soldiers guarding the prisoners understood their language (though they did not realize it). At length he came to Menéndez.

"They talk only to find a way to induce you to land," he said, "so that the archers will have you and your men within range. Saturiba has many warriors waiting in ambush."

"Bring the prisoners back aboard," Menéndez ordered reluctantly. To the interpreter he said, "Have Saturiba told that I have always wanted to be his friend. But from now on, Saturiba must call me his enemy. To avenge my people that he has killed, I will order his head to be cut off, or have him driven out of the country."

Saturiba heard the message and proved his diplomatic experience by sending back far better insults than he had received.

"Why don't you land and fight?" he jibed. "You and your soldiers are hens and cowards!"

Menéndez ignored the insults and swallowed his disappointment at the failure to bring Saturiba into council. He crossed the bar and went on to St. Augustine as planned. There he and the captains agreed on the nature of the offensive to be used against Saturiba; and Menéndez gave specific instructions to build seven blockhouses between Matanzas and Guale. These would be manned by small garrisons. The one near Matanzas was to serve also as a coastal watch station, whence ships could be reported to St. Augustine by courier. The war dogs would be loosed at night to guard against Indians and protect the cattle.

With his usual optimism, however, he hoped to put a finish to the war before he left for Spain. A four-target raid was carefully planned and executed. Menéndez himself led a contingent of seventy men.

But Saturiba eluded them again, and Menéndez tried another tactic. He struck the chains from Emoloa and the other Timucua captives. Through the interpreter, he spoke to Emoloa.

"I go now to Spain, my country far across the sea," he said. "Three notable men from the land of Tequesta go with me. Also I want to take three of you. One will be the son of Emoloa."

Emoloa's face was impassive.

"Your son and his companions will be well treated," Menéndez explained, "and I will bring them back. You and the others are free. Go to Saturiba, your father. Tell him if he or any of you makes war on us, I will cut off the heads of your son and the two others."

Emoloa could do nothing but bid his son farewell.

The wind blew fair, and two vessels nosed out of the harbor. On the third day, Captain Juan Pardo welcomed them at Santa Elena. Brave Pardo had led an expedition deep inland to establish a base amongst friendly natives. A letter with news of the great French armada, seemingly bound for the Indies, had brought him back to defend Santa Elena. Menéndez listened eagerly to his report of the trip to the west. It promised well for the future.

Captain General of the Ocean Sea

HE TRIP to Spain could wait no longer, for it was said that the King would soon be gone to Flanders again. They left Santa Elena May 18, 1567, in a new *fragata*. She was a remarkable galley-type vessel, sturdy enough for deep water and also very fast. Menéndez counted on this speed and the sweeps she carried along with the sail to show her heels to the corsairs they were likely to find beyond the Azores.

Not that they were defenseless, by any means. The *fragata* mounted three small bronze cannon, and most of the twenty-five gentlemen aboard had brought arquebuses or other firearms. Even without arms, their aspect was enough to terrorize an adversary. Ragged, sun-bronzed, strong, they had the look of men who had lived with hardship and violence and death for many months. As indeed they had.

Twenty-five gentlemen! There was young Valdés, who had led the attack on Fort Caroline; Castañeda, the captain of Menéndez' guards; Miranda, Menéndez' son-in-law; and the rest, most of whom were long-time companions of their leader. Good soldiers they were, and sailors, too, for many of them were expert navigators.

In fact, the *fragata* carried only five sailors. Two of these had the additional talent of performing on the trumpet. The six Indians and two prisoners brought the total aboard to thirty-eight souls.

The log showed an amazing average of seventy-two leagues per day; and in seventeen days they sighted the Azores. Going on, they touched Spain at Vivero and continued to Avilés.

The news of their coming preceded them. The people of Avilés were waiting as the tiny *fragata* came up the estuary with pennants and banners flying. The gunners fired the cannon, and the gentlemen loaded the arquebuses and touched them off. The trumpets sounded, again and again. There were shouts of joy, and cries of welcome. And many dropped to their knees,

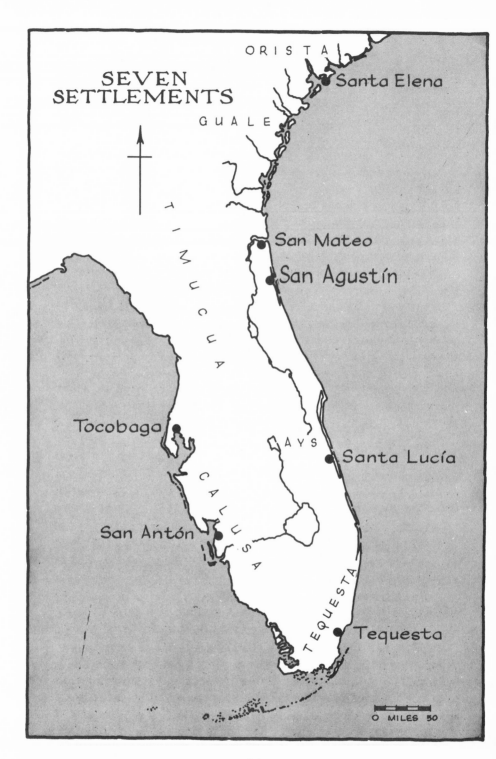

ORISTA

SEVEN
SETTLEMENTS
• Santa Elena

GUALE

TIMUCUA

San Mateo
•San Agustín

Tocobaga•
AYS
•Santa Lucía

CALUSA

San Antón•

TEQUESTA
•Tequesta

O MILES 50

raising their hands to heaven, praising God for his care of this son of Avilés and his company.

But as the craft came closer and those on shore began to see the strange, ragged soldiers and the dark-skinned naked Indians, they stared and became quiet.

Menéndez stepped onto the landing and his comrades followed. The crowd parted. As was his custom, he led the way directly to the church, and knelt to give thanks for a safe voyage. When he came out, the people escorted him to his house, where Ana María and their daughters were waiting, along with his sisters and their children. It was a happy homecoming, this day in July 1567, and an occasion that came only too rarely. For during eighteen years in the King's service, Menéndez had been home only four times.

Nor was this stay a long one. Some of his gentlemen also visited their families before making the long trip with him over the mountains a few days later to Madrid. They arrived at the Court on July 20.

Menéndez delighted Philip by presenting the six Indians in their native dress (which consisted essentially of tattooing, a bow, and quiver of arrows). The audience turned out well, despite defamations that had been circulated by Osorio and others, including the Florida deserters. If the King was ever made doubtful of his man by the glib statements of deserters intent upon saving their own hides, a few minutes with Menéndez drove the doubts from the royal mind.

Against the frustrated anger of the rulers of France, Philip had long ago justified Menéndez' deeds in destroying the French colony. He listened now with interest as Menéndez related his adventures and spoke of affairs in this newest of the royal domains. He told of the march to Fort Caroline, the death of Ribault and the others. He described the land, and the discovery of two dozen harbors along three hundred leagues of coast, their entrances all sounded and marked; and he expounded upon the Indians and their ways, and how there were treaties of friendship with all — except Saturiba. Seven settlements had been made: St. Augustine, San Mateo, Santa Elena, Ays, Tequesta, Carlos, and Tocobaga; and of these the first three were in harbors chosen as suitable refuge for vessels of the treasure fleet. The others were well situated to aid castaways along the dangerous coast, as well as to establish the Faith among the natives.

He touched on the brave loyalty of the soldiers and colonists, the hardships and dangers of the wilderness, and the desperate need for supplies. Nor did he neglect matters in the Caribbean, specifically the deeds of the corsairs and the obligation to punish them.

Philip ordered help sent to the colonies at once, and directed Menéndez to prepare a memorandum on Florida and Caribbean matters for guidance of the Council of the Indies (a thing which he did a few days later).

While he had the ear of the King, Menéndez talked of his plans for Florida. The survey vessels had sailed great distances along the coasts and exploring parties had marched endless leagues, but the unfolding of this vast unknown territory was only just begun. Much was to be learned; strange nations reached; resources discovered.

Most intriguing of all to Philip was Menéndez' conviction that Chesapeake Bay was the Atlantic opening to the fabled Northwest Passage — the short route to the Pacific and the Orient.

Obviously this was a thing that should be determined as soon as possible. There was no time to lose if one believed the rumors of Portuguese settlement in Newfoundland. Menéndez did not hesitate to detail this hearsay: for two years these rivals had been settled on the coast and were now building fortifications inland that would control the Northwest Passage. They must be driven out. If the details contributed little to the truth of the matter, at least they gave it exciting urgency. Neither did Menéndez fail to hammer home the danger of corsairs in Spain's American lake, the Caribbean. When all was added together it came to a crisis.

To meet this exigency, Philip did a characteristic thing: he created a new title, Captain General of the West. And this he gave to Menéndez.

With the title went the charge to secure the Indies against all enemies. To do the job, the Captain General was allotted 200,000 ducats, 2,000 soldiers, and twelve galleons.

In January 1568 Philip elevated him in the Order of Santiago by conferring the Commandery of the Holy Cross of Zarza. This honor meant a yearly income of some eight hundred crowns. Other rewards were to come, not the least of which was victory over Osorio, his enemy in Havana. Osorio was dismissed from office. Menéndez himself was named Governor of Cuba in his place.

The immediate concern, however, was getting a fleet ready to take Philip to Flanders. Menéndez spent February on the Biscayan coast at this task. Then Philip changed his mind about going to Flanders, leaving Menéndez free to bend his energies toward the work cut out for him in America.

Naturally one of his first efforts was to arrange for an increase in the mission work among the Indians. The Jesuits responded. Four priests and ten brothers were appointed. Meanwhile, several of the visiting Indians had been baptised. Together, friars and converts sailed from San Lucar for Florida on March 13, 1568.

In June, the news reached Spain that San Mateo was destroyed. A French force led by Dominique de Gourgues had gone to Florida secretly. Saturiba welcomed De Gourgues gladly, and his warriors joined the French to overwhelm the garrison. The Spanish who survived the assault were hanged.

The jobs Philip had given him to do kept Menéndez overlong in Spain. It was late summer before he reached Havana.

There he found most of the Jesuits who had been assigned to Florida; and from their leader, Father Juan Bautista de Segura, he had a discouraging report. They had gone, as planned, to St. Augustine, arriving on June 29 (1568). The people were in rags, hungry and utterly forlorn. San Mateo had just been lost. Help expected from Spain had not come. The Jesuits gave out the little supply of food and clothing they had brought, and concluded that the hunger-ridden colony was not yet able to support missionaries.

Father Segura sent two of the brothers north into the Guale country. He and the others returned south, for he was excited with a plan to start a school at Havana. It would be a place where Floridians — both white and red — could send their children for instruction. Perhaps later, when economics permitted, the religious could go back to the work in Florida.

Father Rogel, from Charlotte Harbor, was also in Havana. Carlos was dead, he told Menéndez. The soldiers had done it. Kill or be killed, that's what it came to. Carlos had become ever more dangerous since Menéndez had forced him into the peace with Tocobaga. So at last they destroyed him. But the colony was still in mortal danger, and Father Rogel had come to Havana to beg alms for the mission, and find aid for the colonists.

At Tequesta, a little progress had been made. Brother Francisco Villareal had learned the language and made a number of conversions. Then for some petty reason the soldiers killed the cacique's uncle. The reprisal was swift and terrible.

Those who survived it fled north to their countrymen at the blockhouse of Ays. Here the drain upon the meager food supply was too much. Not long afterward, Ays was abandoned.

The news of Tocobaga was equally bad. The Indians had slain all the garrison.

Thus Menéndez found that of the seven settlements, four were destroyed: San Mateo, Aÿs, Tequesta and Tocobaga. The others were in danger. But his new responsibilities in Cuba and the Caribbean kept him from the work so badly needed in Florida.

He did what he could. A third missionary was sent to join the two already in Guale. Two others went to Charlotte Harbor. The mission at Tequesta, abandoned after the bloody uprising against the soldiers, was reestablished by Father Segura and Tequesta's brother. The latter was one of those Menéndez had taken to Spain. Now his return as a neophyte in the Faith caused his people to receive the Jesuit in peace, if not exactly with enthusiasm.

By September 1569 Menéndez was back in Spain. It was now four years since the founding of the colony, but it was nowhere close to self-sufficiency. The rents and produce out of which Menéndez was to draw his salary as Florida Governor and pay his royal partner were nonexistent.

More money and people must go into Florida before it could become an economic asset. Menéndez had committed all his fortune. He could not afford to abandon the project. Yet he had no more funds for it, aside from what he cleared in the new jobs Philip had given him.

Since his resources were proving too small for the work, Menéndez tried hard to convince Philip of Florida's strategic importance to Spain. His letters from Sevilla and Cádiz late in 1569 report the growing strength of the corsairs against the pitifully thin line of the King's soldiers in the new province. He chafed at the slowness of the *Casa* in getting his fleet supplied and provisioned. Maintenance of the King's soldiers was the responsibility of the Crown, and Menéndez hoped Philip would castigate the officials who failed to release the necessary provisions, pay and equipment.

"The soldiers Your Majesty has in Florida are not provided for," he stated bluntly. "I have been supporting them for days at my own expense. They consume the provisions I sent for the farmers."

THE SISTER CITIES: Avilés (top) and St. Augustine

Before he could leave Spain, it was the new year of 1570. The corsair "Peg Leg" and others were audacious, and Menéndez was at sea a good part of the time, convoying the treasure fleets between the Canaries and Spain. Ashore, the affairs of Cuba and Florida kept him occupied, even at a distance.

The reports from Florida were now continually bad. The Charlotte Harbor settlement at last was abandoned, after another break with the Indians; the garrison moved to St. Augustine. The same happened again at Tequesta. The Jesuit school at Havana, which was staffed with the missionaries intended for Florida, did not flourish, so Father Segura had taken them to join the others at Guale and Santa Elena. The promising start there was wiped out by a revolt among the Gualeans, who grew resentful of the gaunt, half-starved soldiers who came to collect levies of corn. At St. Augustine, the situation did not improve; the place was still troubled with desertions and mutiny.

The only bright spot was the report that eight of the Jesuit fathers had sailed in August to begin a mission among the Indians of Chesapeake Bay.

After December 1570, Menéndez was again in Spain. Philip licensed him to recruit a hundred more farmers for Florida, and for the next several months he was busy putting together another sizeable expedition. As usual, the *Casa* officials gave trouble; weather delayed the sailing; a ship was lost; but at last the little armada sailed from San Lucar on May 17. It numbered seven galleons, two hundred and fifty soldiers and sailors, and four hundred other souls.

They reached Havana July 3, 1571. The treasure fleet was still in the harbor, and Menéndez at once found himself involved in readying the armed vessels that would escort the fleet back to Spain. There were many other responsibilities, of course. Some of his people were sick, and had to be put ashore for treatment. There were also the usual desertions among those whose appetite for adventure had been dulled by the hardship of the ocean crossing, or whose true objective had been the warm promise of the Caribbean rather than the hostile wilderness of Florida.

There was also a disturbing report on the failure of the Jesuit mission on the Chesapeake. Menéndez gave another the task of leading the convoy to Spain, and set out for Florida at once. After a brief stop at Santa Elena to land supplies and replacements, he hurried on to the Chesapeake. There was little hope of finding any of the missionaries alive; but perhaps he could learn how they died, and chastise their executioners.

On the shores of the Chesapeake there was no sign of human life. Menéndez debarked with a company of men to search out the Indians, and had the incredible luck to capture eight of them and rescue a small Spanish boy named Alonso, son of a settler at Santa Elena. The child had served the Jesuit fathers as altar boy. All the others were dead.

According to Alonso, the eight Indian captives had been members of the war party that killed the missionaries. Menéndez forthwith ordered them hanged from the ship's yardarm.

There was no time to search for the bones of the dead missionaries and give them a decent burial. In the other colonies, the living clamored for attention; and since the storm season was already at hand, Menéndez was anxious to start back for Santa Elena.

It was well into December before he reached St. Augustine. He stayed long enough to land the people and the cargoes and leave some of his own enthusiasm with the colonists, then on December 20 embarked again for Havana with a little fleet consisting of a bark and two smaller vessels. Despite the weather risk, he would not stay the winter in Florida when he was needed in the Caribbean.

This time, however, luck deserted him. He was in one of the smaller boats, which carried about thirty men. A storm swept upon them; and they, like the French had been, were blown onto the beach some thirty leagues south of St. Augustine. Perhaps Menéndez remembered Ribault's words: *What has happened to me could happen to you . . .*

Miraculously they saved their arquebuses and some dry powder. With these, and by using the wreckage as a fort, they beat off attacks by the Indians, who gathered like wolves.

When darkness came, Menéndez led his people swiftly northward. They found canoes to cross the inlets, and courage to resist the Indians who bedevilled them. At last tney reached St. Augustine. Not a man had been lost.

As it turned out, they were a welcome reinforcement. Several days later, English vessels attacked the little settlement, but a determined show of resistance discouraged the raiders.

The accident had left Menéndez a sailor without a ship, chafing at the delay in his plans and impatient to get on with his work. Yet perhaps this enforced stay in Florida, waiting for rescue from Havana, was a disguised blessing. Restless, he had never taken time in the land to savor its gifts: myriads of birds

THE SHORE OF THE "OCEAN SEA"
Portions of the Florida beaches, which Menéndez trod, remain unchanged.

along shores teeming with life; morning's dew heavy on the grasses; the crisp winter air laden with the fragrance of myrtle and bay, cedar and palm, or the acrid pungency of pitch-pine smoke; the warm sun in a blue and cloudless sky.

Let him enjoy it now, for he will never return.

On Good Friday he came at last to Havana and the necessary round of conferences and inspections in the Antilles. The record indicates that he returned to Spain with the treasure fleet in this summer of 1572.

The Florida project was never out of mind, and the extent of his work on it is measurable by the number of cédulas affecting Florida, which Philip signed. One of the most significant enlarged the Florida grant westward to the Pánuco River and Mexico. Philip issued this order on January 23, 1573.

Yet it was not Menéndez' intention to begin a new project before the old one had stability. To discover and set forth certain essential facts, he instructed Menéndez Marqués, his kinsman, to undertake a comprehensive survey of the Atlantic coast from the Keys to the Chesapeake. This was done in the summer of 1573. And though explorations in Chesapeake Bay did not uncover the Northwest Passage, coastal probings elsewhere rescued a number of castaways.

Further matter of concern was agriculture. In 1572 Santa Elena had only about thirty farmers, and St. Augustine a dozen. To improve this situation, Menéndez sent others as often as he could afford to do so.

Religion was another aspect of his Florida work. He was confirmed in the belief that soldiers never made missionaries; and although the Jesuits were gone from the field, the Franciscans were willing to make a start. On February 23, 1573, Philip authorized the passage of six friars. They were working in Florida before the year was out.

As Captain General of the West, Menéndez was never out of touch with naval affairs and the continuous effort to control the corsairs. They seemed to wax stronger as the treasure fleet cargoes grew in value. English vessels were becoming more numerous and their crews bolder, and it was rumored that Philip would soon make up a powerful fleet to deal with this menace.

And indeed on February 10, 1574, Pedro Menéndez was named Captain General of a great armada. Word was given out that it would sail to clear corsairs from the western coast and the way to Flanders; but some smiled knowingly, sure that England was the destination. Else what need for so many ships and men?

It seems to have been about this time Philip had Menéndez sit for the painter Titian, so that his likeness might be placed in the palace gallery along with other illustrious leaders and conquistadores. The *Adelantado* of Florida was now fifty-five years old and at the height of his career. Philip had the utmost confidence in him. High officials looked to him for advice.

The summer of 1574 seemed busier than ever for Menéndez; and as the time came for the armada to be placed formally in his hands, he was a weary man. Heavy-hearted despite the honors that had come to him, he composed a letter to Menéndez Marqués, who was his administrator in Florida:

"The work here is unbearable," he wrote. "After the salvation of my soul, there is nothing in this world I want more than to be in Florida, to end my days saving souls."

He continued: "When I told His Majesty of my unhappiness at being away from Florida, he said he will gladly give me leave whenever it is possible."

His letter informed Marqués that a number of new people had been enlisted for the colony. They were well-trained stone-cutters, carpenters, tradesmen, and the like, who would be useful anywhere, in Florida or Pánuco.

In a burst of enthusiasm, he instructed Marqués, "When you get this letter, plan to come across and see me. I am certain to be at Madrid in March or April . . . and if I am free, we can go back to Florida together."

The letter was written on September 7, 1574. The next day the cannon salutes sounded and the ceremonies began. The King's officials delivered the charge of the armada to Pedro Menéndez, its Captain General, and there was great rejoicing. All the people knew Menéndez, for this was the harbor of Santander, not far from Avilés, the town where he was born.

It was a wonderful day indeed, and a real honor to command this tremendous armada of a hundred and fifty vessels and twelve thousand soldiers and sailors. The masts and spars made a great forest of seapower upon the blue water of the fjord-like harbor.

But Menéndez felt the fever in his veins, and the fire raged throughout a body that was weakened by long months of strain in preparing this ultimate weapon for his King.

SAN NICOLÁS (AVILÉS)
In this old church is the tomb of Menéndez.

In the moments when his mind was clear, regretfully he put Florida out of his thoughts, for certain other things could no longer wait. He received the sacraments and made his will, wherein he asked Philip for the reward promised him after thirty-two years of service. For he had no other way to satisfy his debts. On September 17, 1574, he died.

EPILOGUE

Pedro Menéndez de Avilés y Alonso de la Campa (which is the full name of Florida's founder) was fifty-five years old when he died. For most of those years he was a sailor. His career took him from teen-age recruit to Admiral, then to *Adelantado*, colonial administrator, and finally Captain General of Spain's mightiest fleet. In those days, a lifetime in the King's service meant plenty of action, including combat.

France, the traditional rival of his country, was involved in this career from start to finish. Frenchmen who were relentless in battle against Spain, whether in land armies or as corsairs on the sea, were teachers as well as inspiration for his hatred of Spain's enemies. In countless conflicts he learned their ways. That he survived this perilous school of experience at all is proof of unusual ability. More important, by having acquired respect for their courage — respect which never crumbled into fear, he outlived his teachers.

His military talent was manifest at an early age, and along with it grew two related faculties. One was aptitude as a leader of men; the other, competence as an administrator. Long years of supervising the logistics of the armadas testify to the latter. As to leadership, it is obvious that consistent victories in battle cannot be won without it.

However, it is the Florida enterprise which most clearly shows us the man and what he could do.

As a soldier, he accomplished the Florida mission with brilliance. Against great odds, he removed the threat of the enemy settlement without significant loss to his own forces. His objective was to destroy French capability in Florida. This was accomplished quite simply, as it turned out, by exterminating the French army. Militarily, there was no other way. To begin with, Ribault's men were entrenched and numerically superior, and they came at the first opportunity to attack him at St. Augustine; and when he found them divided and struck them at Fort Caroline and Matanzas, he could neither house nor feed so many captives.

So he killed them. Decisions equally objective, and on a considerably larger scale, have been made in our own times; we of the atomic age may not cry shame at Menéndez.

I do not believe religion was a primary influence in these military decisions. The Frenchmen died because they were a physical threat, not alone to Menéndez and his people, but to Spain's commerce and sovereignty in America. True, the captives at Matanzas were given a chance to disavow the "new religion." But remember also that women and children at Fort Caroline were spared without regard to their religion; and spared too were the men at the wreck of the *Trinity*, in spite of the risk of spiritual contamination to their captors, a risk that Menéndez as a sort of public health officer was bound to abhor.

As planner and executive of the Florida project, Menéndez exhibited large talent. The composition of the colony (farmers, craftsmen, tradesmen, sailors, soldiers and administrators) was good, though reality never really caught up to the plans. The scheme to make settlements at several key harbors was sound. Of course, such commonsensical planning was to be expected. After all, Spaniards had already planted some two hundred colonies in the Americas.

For those of us who consider the vast distances of the sixteenth century, Menéndez surprises us with his mobility. In fact, the man moves with such celerity from place to place that it is difficult to keep the narrative straight. There was not, however, any confusion in Menéndez' mind; his travels invariably had purpose.

Florida reveals yet another aspect of this man: his faith in God. This faith, alive and strong, was a tremendous factor in his plans and decisions and actions. It is evident in his master plan for Florida. Pastoral care must of course be provided for the colonists and soldiers, but it was equally needful to take Christianity to the Indians. This was a responsibility Menéndez accepted — nay, welcomed — not in a lukewarm, general way, but as a personal matter to be handled with zeal.

Hence, his relations with the Indians were founded upon the principle of a militant Church bringing the Gospel to people who, without it, were condemned. In his view, the lines of communication between Christian and potential Christian had to be kept open regardless of obstacles. Being sure that man is God's agent for the spread of the Faith, he could accept Antonia into his household because the arrangement promised to save many Indian souls, even though it might destroy his own. For he agreed to the act, believing at the same time he must endure divine punishment for this sin; and if in God's plan one man's

97

suffering in eternity were necessary for the salvation of so many, then he was willing to be that man.

In contrast to his harsh judgment upon the French, these things suggest a warm regard for humanity. Indeed, Menéndez was much concerned with people, from loyal follower to heathen Indian, from seaman to mutinous captain. Witness his personal persuasiveness in the council of captains, or in the interminable "talks" with the aborigines. People were his great failures: Osorio, Rodabán, Carlos, Antonia, and the dozens of deserters who slipped away from the Florida service; these were the ones who could not perceive his vision for Florida. But people were also his triumph. Many followed him unto death; others refused to die, but lived on stubbornly and loyally through the hardship and danger, to give Florida a proud Spanish heritage that withstands four hundred years of attrition.

These pages are written because there is, practically speaking, no biography of Pedro Menéndez for the general reader in English. The Founder of Florida and Captain General of the West deserves to be better known.

The record of Pedro Menéndez comes mainly from four sixteenth century sources. They include (1) archival manuscripts, (2) a biography to 1567 by his brother-in-law, Gonzalo Solís de Merás, (3) a second biography by the Salamanca Professor Bartolomé Barrientos, completed in 1568, and (4) the Florida journal of Father Francisco López de Mendoza Grajales, concluded in 1565. The first two have provided most of the material for these pages.

Virtually all the four sources (except for archival documents that escaped the searchers) are published. *La Florida* by Ruidíaz (Madrid 1893) contains many of the known papers, as well as the Merás biography and the narrative by López. The Barrientos manuscript is printed in García's *Dos Antiguas Relaciones de la Florida* (Mexico 1902). All four are also in English translation, excepting numerous documents.* The translations of course vary in quality, but in general tend to multiply the obscurities while simplifying the syntax and redundancies of the old Spanish.

---

*The Merás biography is translated by J. T. Connor under the title *Pedro Menéndez de Avilés* (Gainesville: University of Florida Press, 1964). The Barrientos version, translation by Anthony Kerrigan, bears the title *Pedro Menéndez de Avilés, Founder of Florida* (Gainesville: University of Florida Press, 1965). The López journal is included in B. F. French, *Historical Collections of Louisiana and Florida* (New York: A. Mason, 1875).

Other interesting materials include Barcia's *Historia General de la Florida* (Madrid 1723), put into English by Anthony Kerrigan for the St. Augustine Historical Society (University of Florida Press, 1951). The Menéndez material in Barcia is based upon Merás and seemingly also upon a lost narrative by Menéndez himself. Woodbury Lowery's *The Spanish Settlements* (New York, 1905, and reprinted 1959) is still the best history of early Florida. With a sailor's understanding and the perception of a marine architect, Admiral Julio F. Guillén has written about Spanish naval practice and vessels (*Historia Marítima Española*, Madrid 1961).

Now finally, it hardly needs saying that a brief biography must omit many things. Perhaps these pages will prick your interest and send you to the sources to discover more about Pedro Menéndez de Avilés. I hope so.

Addendum 1985: Since the first edition of *Florida's Menéndez* (1965), Dr. Eugene Lyon has devoted a book to the Florida project of Menéndez: *The Enterprise of Florida: Pedro Menéndez de Avilés and the Spanish Conquest of 1565-1568* (Gainesville: University Presses of Florida, 1976). In this readable 250-page volume, Menéndez' thoughts and actions are conveyed from the archival records to the printed page, and there placed against the backdrop of Spain's colonial and maritime organization and effort. Lyon's book reveals Menéndez as a human being with a fair share of humankind's strengths and foibles, ideals and ambitions; but above all as a man with the courage and resourcefulness to meet the challenge of his times.

Some 16th Century Vessels

Narrow Hulls

Galera. Galley, a warship of the Mediterranean since the times of antiquity. The craft was armed with a ram at the stem and often had bow- and stern-chaser cannon as well. Some of the low, fast, narrow-beamed hulls were 200 feet long and could carry 1,200 men. Speed came from one or more banks of oars manned by slaves. This manpower was supplemented by two or three lateen sails. The full-sized galley had 50 or more benches. Smaller classes included the *galeota*, *fusta*, *bergantín* and *fragata*. Though not designed for trans-ocean sailing, many of them did cross the Atlantic. Countless others were built in the Americas and used for coastal exploration.

Galeota. A galley of medium size. *La Victoria*, with Menendéz on his 1565 voyage to Florida, had 17 benches and a crew of 17. She carried 250 jugs of water, 7½ tons of hardtack, and other provisions.

Bergantín. A small galley. *La Esperanza*, with Menéndez in 1565, had 11 benches and 6 crewmen. *Bergantines* used for exploration of the Florida Keys and the St. Johns River carried from 30 to 50 soldiers. It appears that the sweeps of the American galleys were manned as needed, not by slaves, but by military personnel.

Fragata. Smallest of the galleys. A new *fragata*, seemingly built at Havana to Menéndez' specifications, crossed the ocean to Spain in 1567 with 5 crewmen and 33 others.

Galeaza. Galeass, a vessel larger than a galley, smaller than a galleon, with characteristics of both. While the long hull lines were reminiscent of the galley, the *galeaza* often boasted broadside armament and low castles fore and aft. Some models were oarless. With high freeboard for deepwater navigation, she could carry up to 700 tuns (water casks), or 60 cannon and 1,500 men. Above deck, she was square-rigged like a galleon.

Galeón. Galleon, or large armed vessel used in the transocean trade. The galleon evolved in response to Spain's need for an ocean-crossing cargo ship capable of beating off corsairs. Pedro Menéndez, along with Alvaro de Bazán (the hero of Lepanto), is credited with developing the prototypes which had the long hull — and sometimes the oars — of the galley married to the poop and prow of the *nao* or merchantman. *Galeones* were classed as 1-, 2-, and 3-deckers, and stepped two or more masts rigged with square sails and topsails (except for a lateen sail on the mizzenmast). Capacity ranged up to 900 tuns or more. Menéndez' *San Pelayo* of 1565 was a 900-tun galleon which has also been called a *nao* and *galeaza*. She carried 77 crewmen, 18 gunners, and transported 317 soldiers and 26 families, as well as provisions and cargo. Her armament was iron.

Broad-beamed Ships

Nao, navío. Ship, or seagoing cargo vessel with capacity of 900 tuns or more, two or three masts, and generally square-rigged with topsails. In Menéndez' time, the terms were usually synonymous in designating any principal vessel regardless of type (galleon, hooker, carrack, etc.), but later signified merchantman and warship, respectively. The *San Salvador* bound for Florida in 1565 was called *un navío bueno*.

Caravela. Caravel, a broad-bowed, high-pooped, 3- or 4-masted merchantman capable of loading 100 tuns or more. Of Mediterranean origin, the caravel was usually lateen rigged, but in the Indies trade she was often converted to a square-rigger. The *Sant Antonio* on the 1565 voyage to Florida had a 150-tun capacity, and transported 114 soldiers in addition to her crew and a cargo of provisions.

Smaller Craft

Barco. The **barco** class were coastal freighters and fishermen, built and rigged in various styles. The *barco gavarra* was the largest. She carried main- and foretopsails, and had a cargo capacity of 150 *pipas* (pipes of wine). Smallest was the *barco longo*, with single square sail reminiscent of the Viking ship. An unusual outrigger at the stem aided sail handling. Low freeboard made the craft easy to row.

Patache. Menéndez' first command was his own *patache*, a swift, sturdy row-sailer descended from the *barco longo*, and carrying 50 men on coast patrol. Later, *patache* became a generic name for the small courier and reconnaissance vessels of an armada.

Zabra. A versatile Biscayan row-sailer with space for 100 to 200 tuns. She served equally well as a rough water fisherman, deep sea freighter, or a corsair capable of carrying 150 fighting men across the Atlantic.

Chalupa. Shallop, or swift-sailing, single-decked cargo vessel of 60 to 100 tuns capacity. The *San Miguel* with Menéndez in 1565 carried 9 crewmen, 51 soldiers, and provisions, arms and munitions. She was rated at 60 tuns.

Pinaza. Pinnace, or open row-sailer, between the shallop and longboat in size.

Lancha. Longboat, or open boat with oars and demountable sailing mast. *Lanchas, esquifes* (skiffs) and *botes* (boats) were towed or stowed aboard seagoing vessels as tenders.

See illustrations overleaf →

FRAGATA

BERGANTÍN

GALEAZA

GALEÓN

GALEOTA

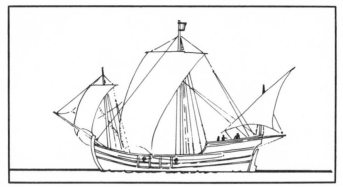

BARCOLONGO

CARAVELA

NAVÍO

Acknowledgement

I am especially grateful to my colleague Luis Rafael Arana of the National Park Service for invaluable technical help and encouragement; to Fr. Michael V. Gannon of the Mission of Nombre de Dios for advice and counsel; to Mrs. Doris Coleman Wiles, staff historian of the St. Augustine Historical Society, for ready assistance at all times; to John Tyler Van Campen, editor of the Society, for skilfully putting the book together; and to my wife Clara and my mother Elizabeth for their proof-reading and patience.

Albert Manucy